SOUTH CAROLINA DMV EXAM WORKBOOK

The Ultimate Guide with 400+ Questions, a Detailed Study Plan, and Bonus Tools for Exam Success

WHY THIS WORKBOOK WORKS

Since our journey began, we've had the privilege of helping thousands of aspiring drivers prepare for their DMV exams. Over 10,000 test-takers have shared their experiences with us, and their feedback has been invaluable in shaping the strategies and resources you'll find in this workbook.

A common theme we've noticed is that many people approach the DMV exam feeling confident but ultimately unprepared, often missing key steps that could ensure their success. On the other hand, those who passed on their first attempt consistently followed a few proven strategies: they engaged in regular, focused practice, utilized a variety of study tools, and thoroughly familiarized themselves with the exam material.

This workbook is designed to replicate those successful strategies, giving you access to practice tests, flashcards, and guides that have helped countless others achieve their goal of obtaining a driver's license. By following the steps laid out in this book, you'll be setting yourself up for success—just like the thousands of test-takers who came before you.

But don't just take our word for it. Here's what some of our satisfied customers have to say:

Ashley Cooper, New Driver
★★★★★
"This book was exactly what I needed to prepare for my test. The practice questions are spot-on, mirroring the actual exam format, and the state-specific focus ensured I was studying all the right material. The explanations made everything so easy to understand, and the extra bonuses, like flashcards and the downloadable handbook, were incredibly helpful. This book isn't just a study guide—it's the best tool out there to help you pass your test with confidence."

Maria Sanchez, Parent of a Teenager

★★★★★

"Helping my son study for the DMV test felt overwhelming until we found this workbook. The questions are clear, the structure is logical, and the state-specific details are perfect for making sure he's learning exactly what he needs to know. The extra practice tests were a huge confidence booster, and I appreciated the 100 FAQs that answered all our lingering questions, also the study plan helped him focus and guided him through the process. This book truly is a one-stop-shop for passing the DMV exam."

John Lee, First-Time Test Taker

★★★★★

"I was really nervous about taking my driving test, but the workbook took the edge off. The practice questions and mock exams were incredibly realistic, and the book's layout made studying so much more manageable. The state-specific focus meant I was getting the exact info I needed, and the added extras like the handbook download were super useful. I couldn't have asked for a better resource to get me ready."

Remember, the key to passing your DMV exam isn't just confidence—it's preparation. With the right approach, you can avoid the pitfalls that catch so many others off guard and join the ranks of those who have passed their exam with flying colors.

INTRODUCTION

Welcome, and thank you for choosing our workbook as your trusted companion on the journey to earning your driver's license. This carefully crafted resource is designed not just as a book but as a comprehensive guide that empowers you with the knowledge, confidence, and practice necessary to excel on your DMV test.

Each question in this workbook is thoughtfully selected and derived directly from your state's Driver's Manual, ensuring that you are studying the most relevant and accurate material. Our goal is to help you fully understand the concepts, so you can turn any uncertainties into strengths, ultimately leading to success on test day.

To get the most out of this workbook, we encourage you to adopt the following general strategies:

1. **Follow the Study Plan:** This workbook includes a detailed study plan designed to guide you step by step through your preparation. By adhering to this plan, you'll ensure that you cover all the necessary material systematically, avoiding any last-minute cramming. The study plan is structured to help you build your knowledge progressively, reinforce what you've learned, and track your progress along the way.
2. **Consistent Practice:** Regular practice is key to retaining information and building your test-taking endurance. Start by taking the practice tests under conditions that closely mimic the actual exam—one sitting, timed, and without interruptions. This will not only assess your current knowledge but also help you get comfortable with the format and timing of the real exam.
3. **Thorough Review:** After completing each practice test, spend time reviewing the questions you answered incorrectly. The answer key, located at the back of the book, provides detailed explanations for each question. Understanding your mistakes is crucial for improvement, as it allows you to correct misunderstandings and reinforces the correct information.
4. **Regular Revision:** To solidify your knowledge, make a habit of revisiting the material periodically. Regular revision helps

reinforce what you've learned and improves your ability to recall information during the exam. Remember, repetition is a powerful tool in the learning process.

5. **Stay Informed:** Driving laws and regulations can change, so it's important to ensure that you're studying the most up-to-date information. While this workbook is current, we recommend periodically checking online resources or contacting your local DMV to confirm there have been no recent changes to the laws in your state.

Remember, success is achieved through persistent and smart preparation. The more you engage with the material, the better you'll understand it, and the more confident you'll be when it's time to take the actual DMV exam.

Each question in this workbook is accompanied by a detailed explanation. In cases where multiple answers may seem correct, we've provided comprehensive explanations to clarify why the correct answer is right and why the others are not. This level of understanding is crucial—it's what differentiates those who merely pass from those who truly excel.

We believe that with dedication, practice, and the right guidance, you can master the skills required to pass the DMV test. This workbook is your roadmap to success. Follow the plan, put in the effort, and you'll be well on your way to becoming a confident and responsible driver.

Good luck on your journey!

Study Plan for Your Exam: A Step-by-Step Guide

Whether you're just starting or refining your knowledge before test day, this step-by-step guide will help you stay organized, focused, and on track. This plan breaks down the preparation process into manageable steps, ensuring that you cover all the essential material and build a solid foundation for success.

By following this guide, you'll be able to track your progress, identify areas where you need extra practice, and approach your exam with the confidence that comes from thorough preparation.

Let's get started on the road to acing your DMV exam!

Step 1: Obtain and Review the DMV Handbook

- **Objective:** Gain a thorough understanding of your state's traffic laws and regulations to form the foundation of your study plan.

- **Action Items:**
    - **Download or Pick Up the DMV Handbook:** Obtain the latest version of your state's DMV handbook. This is your primary study resource, covering all the rules, regulations, and road signs you need to know. You will find both a link and a QR code to download the **OFFICIAL** handbook on the next pages.
    - **Read Through the Handbook:** Schedule dedicated time to read through the entire handbook. It's best to break this into manageable sections (e.g., one chapter per day).
    - **Highlight Key Points:** As you read, use a highlighter or make notes in the margins to mark important information, such as speed limits, right-of-way rules, and specific state regulations.
    - **Create Summary Notes:** After reading each section, summarize the key points in your own words. This will reinforce your learning and create a quick reference guide for later review.

- **Progress Tracking:**
- Handbook obtained.
- Completed reading each section of the handbook.
- Highlighted key information.
- Created summary notes for quick reference.

Step 2: Take a Baseline Practice Test

- **Objective:** Establish a starting point by assessing your current knowledge and identifying areas that need improvement.

- **Action Items:**
    - **Complete the First 2 Practice Tests:** Set aside time to take the first 2 practice tests in the workbook. Ensure you simulate real test conditions by timing yourself and avoiding any outside help.
    - **Review Your Results:** After completing the test, carefully review your answers. Identify which questions you got wrong and understand why the correct answers are correct.
    - **Identify Weak Areas:** Make a list of the topics or question types where you struggled the most. This list will guide your focused study sessions in the next steps.

- **Progress Tracking:**
- Baseline practice tests completed.
- Results reviewed and analyzed.
- Weak areas identified.

Step 3: Review Road Signs and Traffic Signals

- **Objective:** Ensure that you can recognize and understand all road signs and traffic signals, which are crucial components of the DMV test.

- **Action Items:**
  - **Flashcards:** Practice with the online flashcards with images of road signs on one side and their meanings on the other. You can find the **link to the flashcards** in the Road Sign section and in the resources page.
  - **Study the Road Signs Section in the Workbook:** Carefully review the 50 questions and their explanations in the workbook's Road Signs and Signs and Situations sections to ensure you fully understand the meanings of all road signs.
  - **Practice Recognition:** Look for opportunities to identify road signs while driving or walking around your neighborhood. This real-world practice can reinforce what you've learned.

- **Progress Tracking:**
- Road Signs and Traffic Signals sections studied.
- Flashcards regularly reviewed.
- Real-world practice conducted.

Step 4: Take a Full-Length Timed Practice Test

- **Objective:** Simulate the real test environment to assess your readiness under pressure and ensure you're comfortable with the time constraints, by now you should have a solid understanding of key concepts.

- **Action Items:**
    - **Complete All Remaining Sections of the Workbook:** Make sure to work through any remaining sections of the workbook besides the Practice Test 3 and the Mock Test
    - **Complete Practice Test 3 Under Realistic Conditions:** Approach this practice test as if it were the real DMV exam. Avoid using any aids, and closely monitor your time. This will help you build test-taking stamina and get used to managing time effectively.
    - **Analyze Your Performance:** After completing the test, carefully review your answers to identify any mistakes. Pay special attention to the questions you answered incorrectly or felt uncertain about.

Progress Tracking:

- All remaining workbook sections completed.
- Full-length timed practice test 3 completed.
- Test results reviewed and analyzed.

Step 5: Revise Key Areas and Cheat Sheets

- **Objective:** Refresh your knowledge on the most critical topics, ensuring they are top of mind as your test date approaches.

- **Action Items:**
    - **Top 100 Most Frequently Asked Questions:** Access this resource and review each question thoroughly. These are the questions that appear most often on the test, so becoming familiar with them will increase your chances of success.
    - **Commonly Missed Test Questions:** This section highlights the questions that test-takers often get wrong. By studying these questions, you'll be better prepared to tackle tricky items and avoid common mistakes on the exam.
    - **Revisit Important Sections of the Handbook:** Focus on revising key topics such as speed limits, right-of-way rules, and other essential regulations.
    - **Review Practice Test Mistakes:** Go over the mistakes you made in your practice tests. Ensure you understand why you got them wrong and what the correct answers are.
    - **Final Study Session:** Schedule a dedicated study session a few days before the test to go over all your notes, summaries, and practice questions one last time.

- **Progress Tracking:**
- Important handbook sections revised.
- Practice test mistakes reviewed.
- Final study session completed.
- Top 100 FAQs
- Commonly Missed Test Questions

Step 6: Take a Final Practice Test

- **Objective:** Confirm your readiness by taking one last practice test to ensure you're fully prepared for the actual exam.

- **Action Items:**
  - **Take the Mock Test:** Instead of choosing a random practice test, take the mock test provided in your study resources. Complete it under timed conditions to simulate the actual exam experience.
  - **Aim for 90% or Higher:** Strive to score at least 90% on this final test. This will give you a comfortable margin of error for the actual exam.
  - **Review Any Remaining Weaknesses:** If there are still areas where you're scoring low, take some extra time to review these topics before the exam.
  - **Bonus Questions:** If your score is still below 80%, we recommend downloading the 200 Bonus Questions for additional practice and reinforcement.

- **Progress Tracking:**
- Final practice test completed.
- Achieved target score (90% or higher).
- Remaining weak areas reviewed.

Step 7: Prepare for Test Day

- **Objective:** Ensure you are fully prepared both mentally and logistically for the DMV test.

- **Action Items:**
  - **Get Plenty of Rest:** Make sure to get a good night's sleep before the test day.
  - **Stay Calm and Confident:** On the day of the test, take a few deep breaths, review any key points you feel unsure about, and trust in your preparation.
  - **Review Key Resources:** If time permits, go over the *Top 100 Most Frequently Asked Questions* and *Commonly Missed Test Questions*.
  - **The day before your exam:** Make sure to read the concise guide, "*8 Tips for Guaranteed Success on Your Driving Test*" This resource is packed with practical advice designed to boost your confidence.

- **Progress Tracking:**
- Adequate rest before the test.
- Arrived at the DMV on time and fully prepared.
- Revise the Top 100 FAQs and Commonly Missed Test Questions
- Read the short guide on "8 Tips for Guaranteed Success on Your Driving Test"

Final Thoughts

This detailed study plan is designed to guide you through every step of your DMV exam preparation, ensuring that you're fully equipped to succeed. By following this plan and tracking your progress along the way, you'll build confidence and mastery over the material, setting yourself up for a successful test day.

Remember, consistent effort and focused study are the keys to passing your DMV exam on the first attempt. Good luck!

THE SOUTH CAROLINA DRIVER'S HANDBOOK

The South Carolina Department of Motor Vehicles strongly recommends that all test takers familiarize themselves with the official manual. This comprehensive guide offers an in-depth understanding of the rules, regulations, and knowledge required to pass your exam. It is suggested that you read through this manual at least once to familiarize yourself with the necessary content.

To access this invaluable resource, simply scan the provided QR code or type the link into your browser to download it.

https://driving-tests.org/south-carolina/sc-dmv-drivers-handbook-manual

Additional Study Resources

To further support your preparation, we've included a suite of bonus resources that go beyond the official handbook. These tools are designed to enhance your study experience and help you feel fully prepared on test day. On the next page, you'll find QR codes and links to access the following:

- **Road Sign Flashcards:** An interactive tool to help you master the road signs you'll encounter on the exam.

- **Top 100 FAQs Flashcards:** Flashcards covering the most frequently asked questions on the DMV test.
- **Most Commonly Missed Test Questions:** A guide to the questions that often trip up test-takers, helping you avoid common mistakes.
- **"8 Tips to Pass and You'll Pass. Guaranteed!" Guide:** A practical guide with proven tips to help you pass your DMV exam on the first try.

Simply scan the QR codes or type in your browser the links to access these resources instantly. If you encounter any issues or have questions, feel free to reach out to us at **info@infiniteinkpress.org**—we're here to help!

Your Journey to Success

We are dedicated to helping you succeed in obtaining your driver's license. To maximize your chances of passing the DMV exam, we encourage you to take full advantage of the practice tests and resources provided in this workbook. Consistent practice and thorough review of the material are key to mastering the content and boosting your confidence.

Now is the perfect time to dive into your studies and start your journey toward acing the DMV exam! We're honored that you've chosen this book as your guide, and we're confident that it will help you achieve your driving goals.

Finally, we'd love to hear about your experience with this book. Your feedback is invaluable in helping us improve our resources and better assist future drivers. Please consider leaving a review and sharing your thoughts on your learning journey.

Good luck, and happy studying!

BONUSES & RESOURCES

RESOURCES

We're committed to providing you with the tools and resources you need to succeed on your DMV exam. Below, you'll find links and QR codes to access our exclusive online bonuses, designed to enhance your study experience and boost your confidence as you prepare for the test.

1. Road Sign Flashcards

Mastering road signs is essential for both the written and practical parts of your DMV exam. Our interactive Road Sign Flashcards are designed to help you quickly and effectively learn and retain the meanings of various road signs.

- **Access the Road Sign Flashcards:** expert-driving-school.webflow.io

2. Top 100 FAQs Flashcards

We've compiled the top 100 most frequently asked questions on the DMV exam and turned them into flashcards to help you test your knowledge and ensure you're ready for any question that might come your way.

- **Access the Top 100 FAQs Flashcards:**
  expert-driving-school.webflow.io/flashcards-dmv-questions

3. Most Commonly Missed Test Questions

Avoid common pitfalls with our guide to the Most Commonly Missed Test Questions. This resource will help you focus on the areas where test-takers typically struggle, giving you an advantage on exam day.

- **Access the Most Commonly Missed Test Questions:**
  https://bit.ly/Missed-Questions

4. "8 Tips for Guaranteed Success on Your Driving Test!" Guide

Our "8 Tips for Guaranteed Success on Your Driving Test" guide is packed with practical advice and proven strategies to help you ace your DMV exam. Follow these tips, and you'll set yourself up for success.

- **Access the "8 Tips for Guaranteed Success on Your Driving Test" Guide:**
  https://bit.ly/DMV-Guaranteed

200 BONUS PRACTICE QUESTIONS

"Bonus Practice Questions" is a comprehensive collection of additional, carefully crafted questions that mirror the variety, style, and complexity of the ones you'll encounter in the real DMV exam. Perhaps you've already completed the questions in our main guide and are yearning for more practice. Or maybe you just want to challenge yourself and ensure no stone is left unturned in your preparations. Regardless of your motivation, this bonus eBook is your perfect ally.

To retrieve this resource, simply enter the provided link into your browser or make use of the QR Code for swift access.

https://dl.bookfunnel.com/l15oxwpd9e

How to Use These Resources

- **Scan the QR Codes:** Simply point your smartphone camera at the QR code for instant access to the resource. This feature is especially useful if you're on the go.
- **Click the Links:** If you're reading this on a digital device, you can click the hyperlinks to be taken directly to the resources.
- **Bookmark the Pages:** Save the links in your browser or add them to your favorites so you can return to these valuable tools whenever you need a quick review.

If you encounter any problem, please send us an email at **info@infiniteinkpress.org** we will be happy to help you!

PRACTICE TEST 1

Prepare for the DMV driving permit test by practicing with questions that closely resemble (and are almost identical to) those you'll encounter on the actual DMV exam. We strongly recommend that you go through each question, time yourself, and only review your answers after completing the entire practice test. The answers can be found in the last section of the book.

Total Questions: 40
Correct Answer to pass: 32

Question 1 - Practice Test 1

What should you do if you see a pedestrian crossing where there's no marked crosswalk or traffic signal?

- ☐ Alert the pedestrian and proceed cautiously
- ☐ Activate your hazard lights and proceed cautiously
- ☐ Give the pedestrian the right-of-way
- ☐ Continue at a slow pace since there's no traffic signal

Question 2 - Practice Test 1

If you accidentally pass your intended turn at an intersection, what should you do next?

- ☐ Halt
- ☐ Execute a U-turn
- ☐ Move on to the next intersection
- ☐ Reduce your speed

Question 3 - Practice Test 1

If a U-turn isn't possible due to limited space, what kind of turn should you make?

- ☐ A five-point turn
- ☐ A three-point turn
- ☐ A four-point turn
- ☐ A two-point turn

Question 4 - Practice Test 1

What sequence should you follow when checking for traffic at an intersection?

- ☐ Left-left-right pattern
- ☐ Left-right pattern
- ☐ Right-left-right pattern
- ☐ Left-right-left pattern

Question 5 - Practice Test 1

Doubling your speed on a highway will increase your braking distance by how much?

- ☐ Fivefold
- ☐ Fourfold
- ☐ Threefold
- ☐ Twofold

Question 6 - Practice Test 1

Headrests should be adjusted to contact the back of your head in order to prevent what?

- ☐ Neck injuries from rear-end collisions
- ☐ Physical injuries in frontal collisions
- ☐ Rear-end accidents
- ☐ Seatbelt tightening during crashes

Question 7 - Practice Test 1

What does it mean if there are two continuous yellow lines in the middle of the road?

- ☐ Overtaking is forbidden in both directions
- ☐ Overtaking is allowed in both directions
- ☐ Overtaking is allowed for larger vehicles
- ☐ Overtaking is allowed in one direction

Question 8 - Practice Test 1

Which statement about freeway interchanges is incorrect?

- ☐ The two primary types of interchanges are diamond and cloverleaf
- ☐ If you miss your exit, utilize a median crossover to reverse course
- ☐ If you take the wrong exit, you must complete the interchange
- ☐ If you miss your exit, proceed to the next one

Question 9 - Practice Test 1

How should you enter a roundabout, regardless of the direction you intend to go?

☐   Turn left, then turn left again

☐   Turn left, then turn right

☐   Turn right and blend into the traffic

☐   Turn left and blend into the traffic

Question 10 - Practice Test 1

If another vehicle is overtaking you, what should you do?

☐   Shift to the right lane and maintain your speed

☐   Stay in your current lane and do not increase your speed

☐   Speed up

☐   Shift to the left lane

Question 11 - Practice Test 1

What purpose do mile markers serve when placed along the outside shoulder of a road?

☐   To indicate upcoming highways

☐   To describe the road's condition

☐   To show the speed limits of the road

☐   To inform drivers of their current location

Question 12 - Practice Test 1

What is the term for the arrangement of ramps connecting a freeway to another road or freeway?

- ☐ Interchange
- ☐ Entry ramp
- ☐ Exit ramp
- ☐ Acceleration lane

Question 13 - Practice Test 1

Why should you avoid driving beside other cars on multilane roads?

- ☐ You may lose sight of the cars ahead
- ☐ You may get rear-ended
- ☐ You may lose sight of trailing cars
- ☐ Your lane might get encroached upon

Question 14 - Practice Test 1

What should you NOT do when driving through a work zone?

- ☐ Maintain pace with other cars
- ☐ Look out for lower speed limits
- ☐ Weave from lane to lane
- ☐ Decelerate your speed

Question 15 - Practice Test 1

What should you do if you encounter a yield sign in your lane?

- ☐ Shift to the left lane
- ☐ Pull over to the side
- ☐ Slow down and stop if needed
- ☐ Speed up

Question 16 - Practice Test 1

If your parked car accidentally rolls away and strikes another unoccupied parked car, what should you do?

- ☐ Reposition your car and find a more secure spot
- ☐ Leave an identifying note
- ☐ Move your car and continue on your way
- ☐ Repair the other vehicle

Question 17 - Practice Test 1

When exiting a high-speed, two-lane road, what should you avoid doing if you have traffic following you?

- ☐ Brake abruptly
- ☐ Refrain from decelerating suddenly
- ☐ Decelerate as quickly as possible
- ☐ Speed up

Question 18 - Practice Test 1

During a turn, the rear wheels of any vehicle will follow a path that is _____ than that of the front wheels.

- ☐ faster
- ☐ shorter
- ☐ slower
- ☐ longer

Question 19 - Practice Test 1

If you experience a tire blowout, what should you NOT do?

- ☐ Firmly hold the steering wheel
- ☐ Brake instantly
- ☐ Steer in a straight line
- ☐ Gradually lift your foot off the gas pedal

Question 20 - Practice Test 1

If no traffic control signals are present, you must slow down or stop for pedestrians _____.

- ☐ at an unmarked crosswalk
- ☐ at an intersection
- ☐ at a marked crosswalk
- ☐ all of the above

Question 21 - Practice Test 1

If your car's engine fails while you're on a bend, what's the best course of action?

☐   Try reactivating the engine while on the road

☐   Steer your car to the right side of the street

☐   Maintain a firm grip on the wheel and proceed straight ahead

☐   Slowly lift off the gas pedal

Question 22 - Practice Test 1

When a median or barrier divides a highway into two separate lanes, _____.

☐   do not cross the barrier unless at a designated crossover point

☐   only cross the barrier for a U-turn

☐   you may cross the barrier for a left-hand turn

☐   crossing the barrier is permitted in emergency situations

Question 23 - Practice Test 1

On a multi-lane road going in one direction, which lanes generally allow for the smoothest traffic flow?

☐   The right-most lane

☐   Acceleration lanes

☐   The left-most lane

☐   The central lanes

Question 24 - Practice Test 1

Why should you reduce your speed when driving on a dirt or gravel road?

☐   Your vehicle will accumulate more dirt at higher speeds

☐   Fast driving on such surfaces is uncomfortable

☐   The windshield may get covered in dirt

☐   You'll experience reduced traction

Question 25 - Practice Test 1

What are the regions around large vehicles like trucks where other cars may not be visible called?

☐   No-Zones

☐   Blind-Zones

☐   Side-Zones

☐   Slow-Zones

Question 26 - Practice Test 1

Before reversing your car, you should look to the front, sides, and rear, and keep looking _____ while backing up?

☐   to the sides

☐   in your side-view mirrors

☐   straight ahead

☐   to the rear

Question 27 - Practice Test 1

If there is/are _____ next to your lane, you are allowed to pass or switch lanes over those area(s).

- ☐ two continuous yellow lines
- ☐ a continuous white line
- ☐ a continuous yellow line
- ☐ a broken white line

Question 28 - Practice Test 1

What type of parking is often seen in malls and wide city streets?

- ☐ Angle parking
- ☐ Hill parking
- ☐ Parallel parking
- ☐ Emergency parking

Question 29 - Practice Test 1

When overtaking another vehicle, maintain a safe distance and do not do what until the coast is clear?

- ☐ Merge back into your original lane
- ☐ Continue in a straight line
- ☐ Speed up
- ☐ Shift back into the overtaking lane

Question 30 - Practice Test 1

Why are rear-end collisions frequent on highways?

- ☐ Drivers are slow to brake
- ☐ Drivers follow too closely
- ☐ Drivers are often intoxicated
- ☐ Drivers neglect to use their headlights

Question 31 - Practice Test 1

If you arrive first at a crash scene, what should be your next steps?

- ☐ Alert oncoming drivers
- ☐ Contact local law enforcement
- ☐ Relocate your car off the active part of the road
- ☐ Perform all the actions listed above

Question 32 - Practice Test 1

What can you do to reduce skidding while entering a curve?

- ☐ Decrease your speed
- ☐ Accelerate
- ☐ Shift to a higher gear
- ☐ Turn on your headlights

Question 33 - Practice Test 1

How should you manage your speed while going downhill on a steep road?

- ☐ Continuously apply your brakes
- ☐ Press hard on the accelerator
- ☐ Shift to a higher gear
- ☐ Change to a lower gear

Question 34 - Practice Test 1

When switching lanes, all these steps are correct EXCEPT:

- ☐ Check your blind spots by looking over your shoulder
- ☐ Not taking your eyes off the road ahead for more than an instant
- ☐ Turn your steering wheel as you turn your head to check blind spots
- ☐ Use your mirrors for additional perspective

Question 35 - Practice Test 1

If you're 15 or 16 and accrue how many points on your driving record, you'll receive a cautionary letter from the SCDMV?

- ☐ 10 points
- ☐ 6 points
- ☐ 4 points
- ☐ 15 points

Question 36 - Practice Test 1

On a road with multiple lanes in your direction, which lanes should be used for passing?

- ☐ Any lane you prefer
- ☐ A central lane
- ☐ The furthest right lane
- ☐ Either the middle or the left lanes

Question 37 - Practice Test 1

What can unbalanced tires or low tire pressure result in?

- ☐ Better fuel efficiency
- ☐ Quicker tire wear
- ☐ Shorter stopping distance
- ☐ All mentioned effects

Question 38 - Practice Test 1

The distance covered by your vehicle from when you first spot a hazard to when you begin braking is called what?

- ☐ the perception distance
- ☐ the braking distance
- ☐ the stopping distance
- ☐ the reaction distance

Question 39 - Practice Test 1

Before you reach the top of a hill or go into a curve, what should you do?

- ☐   Accelerate and change gears

- ☐   Slow down and move to the road's left side

- ☐   Speed up and turn on your headlights

- ☐   Decelerate and move to the road's right side

Question 40 - Practice Test 1

Which elements affect your vehicle's stopping distance?

- ☐   Reaction distance

- ☐   Perception distance

- ☐   Braking distance

- ☐   All the above listed factors

PRACTICE TEST 2

We strongly recommend that you go through each question, time yourself, and only review your answers after completing the entire practice test. The answers can be found in the last section of the book.

Total Questions: 40
Correct Answer to pass: 32

Question 1 - Practice Test 2

On a hot day, if it begins to rain, be aware that the pavement can become slippery initially. What causes this?

- ☐ Oil from the car
- ☐ Melting of the tires
- ☐ Moisture within the asphalt
- ☐ Oil within the asphalt

Question 2 - Practice Test 2

If a driver has their hand and arm bent at a 90-degree angle and pointing downward, what does it signal?

- ☐ They're about to make a right turn
- ☐ They're slowing down or planning to stop
- ☐ They're going straight
- ☐ They're making a left turn

Question 3 - Practice Test 2

If your vehicle's engine fails while you're maneuvering a curve, what should you do?

☐ Try to restart the engine while on the road

☐ Firmly grip the steering wheel and maintain a straight path

☐ Reduce pressure on the gas pedal

☐ Steer to the right side of the road

Question 4 - Practice Test 2

What offers the best protection in a car crash and serves as the most effective shield against a drunk driver?

☐ A cushion seat

☐ A toolkit

☐ A safety belt

☐ A windshield wiper

Question 5 - Practice Test 2

Why are rear-end collisions a common occurrence on highways?

☐ Drivers often take too long to apply the brakes

☐ Drivers follow too closely

☐ Drivers are under the influence of alcohol

☐ Drivers fail to use their headlights

Question 6 - Practice Test 2

If an oncoming vehicle is in your lane, how can you avoid a head-on collision?

- ☐ Steer left toward the median
- ☐ Keep the steering wheel straight
- ☐ Steer right toward the shoulder or curb line
- ☐ Accelerate

Question 7 - Practice Test 2

A roundabout is a circular intersection in which vehicles travel around a center island in the following direction:

- ☐ Clockwise
- ☐ In a straight line
- ☐ Counterclockwise
- ☐ Any direction

Question 8 - Practice Test 2

What should you do when getting ready to exit a parallel parking spot?

- ☐ Signal your intentions
- ☐ Check your mirrors
- ☐ Look over your shoulder
- ☐ All of the above

Question 9 - Practice Test 2

In the event that your vehicle breaks down on train tracks with a train approaching, what is the appropriate course of action?

☐ Alert the train by opening your doors and signaling

☐ Quickly evacuate the vehicle and move a safe distance away

☐ Attempt to restart the engine

☐ Make an effort to push the vehicle off the tracks

Question 10 - Practice Test 2

When double solid lines are present next to your lane, it means you are:

☐ Not permitted to pass or change lanes

☐ Permitted to pass

☐ Allowed to change lanes

☐ Allowed to make a turn

Question 11 - Practice Test 2

In heavy rain, your car's tires can lose contact with the road by riding on a layer of water. This is known as:

☐ Waterplaning

☐ Rainplaning

☐ Frictionplaning

☐ Hydroplaning

Question 12 - Practice Test 2

When two vehicles encounter each other on a steep mountain road where neither can pass, which vehicle has the right-of-way?

- ☐   Neither of the vehicles
- ☐   The vehicle descending the hill
- ☐   The vehicle ascending the hill
- ☐   The vehicle that arrives first

Question 13 - Practice Test 2

Avoiding panic stops can be achieved by _____.

- ☐   quickly changing lanes
- ☐   applying brakes abruptly
- ☐   identifying hazards well in advance
- ☐   following other vehicles closely

Question 14 - Practice Test 2

If your gas pedal is stuck and you can't free it with your foot, you should _____.

- ☐   continue driving until the gas is depleted
- ☐   apply brakes forcefully
- ☐   switch to neutral gear
- ☐   dial 911 on your mobile phone

Question 15 - Practice Test 2

When you are driving down a steep hill, you should _____.

☐   switch to a higher gear

☐   switch to a lower gear

☐   continually apply the brakes

☐   activate your hazard lights

Question 16 - Practice Test 2

When driving on gravel or dirt, you must reduce your speed because _____.

☐   it's uncomfortable to drive fast

☐   your vehicle will accumulate more dirt at higher speeds

☐   you don't have much traction

☐   the dirt may obscure your windshield

Question 17 - Practice Test 2

If another driver is tailgating you, the best response is to _____.

☐   move to the right lane and stop

☐   move to the left lane and stop

☐   move to the right lane and reduce your speed

☐   move to the left lane and reduce your speed

Question 18 - Practice Test 2

Your braking distance increases by _____ times, if you double your speed on a highway.

- ☐   three
- ☐   two
- ☐   ten
- ☐   four

Question 19 - Practice Test 2

The practice of continually being aware of driving conditions, planning ahead, anticipating hazards, and taking appropriate actions to prevent collisions is known as _____.

- ☐   defensive driving
- ☐   good driving
- ☐   safe driving
- ☐   positive driving

Question 20 - Practice Test 2

When passing another vehicle, you must pass at a safe distance and should NOT _____ until the way is clear.

- ☐   continue in a straight line
- ☐   accelerate
- ☐   move back into the passing lane
- ☐   return to your original lane

Question 21 - Practice Test 2

Faster vehicles should use _____, on a highway with three or more lanes going in one direction.

- ☐ the exit ramp
- ☐ a middle lane
- ☐ the right lane
- ☐ the left lane

Question 22 - Practice Test 2

Your chances of surviving a car crash increase when you use _____ together.

- ☐ the lap belt and shoulder belt
- ☐ the lap belt and a helmet
- ☐ the shoulder belt and hazard flashers
- ☐ none of the above

Question 23 - Practice Test 2

When changing lanes, preparing to pass another vehicle, or merging into traffic, signal and check for passing traffic. First, use your mirrors, then _____.

- ☐ check your vehicle's blind spots
- ☐ inspect the rear of your vehicle
- ☐ check for oncoming traffic
- ☐ check the front of your vehicle

Question 24 - Practice Test 2

On a roadway with three or more lanes traveling in the same direction, which lanes generally offer the smoothest flow of traffic?

- ☐ Acceleration lanes
- ☐ Left lane
- ☐ Right lane
- ☐ Middle lanes

Question 25 - Practice Test 2

Backing up your vehicle in any travel lane should never be done EXCEPT _____.

- ☐ to parallel park
- ☐ at crossroads
- ☐ while making a U-turn
- ☐ at lane crossings

Question 26 - Practice Test 2

You should never drive in the same lane as a motorcycle. Why?

- ☐ The motorcycle requires the entire width of the lane
- ☐ Motorcyclists are not required to respect traffic laws
- ☐ Motorcycles do not have turn signals
- ☐ The motorcycle may lead you astray

Question 27 - Practice Test 2

Vertical rectangular signs with white backgrounds and black letters are typically used as:

- ☐ regulation signs
- ☐ facility signs
- ☐ caution signs
- ☐ directional signs

Question 28 - Practice Test 2

To make a right turn, look left and right, yield the right-of-way, and turn the steering wheel using the technique of:

- ☐ Hand-off-hand
- ☐ the one-handed technique
- ☐ the two-handed technique
- ☐ the hand-over-hand method

Question 29 - Practice Test 2

In which of the following scenarios are you not required to stop completely?

- ☐ When encountering a flashing red traffic light
- ☐ When encountering a stop sign
- ☐ When encountering a steady red traffic light
- ☐ When encountering a flashing yellow traffic light

Question 30 - Practice Test 2

Signs for work zones or construction zones usually have:

- ☐ black letters on an orange background.
- ☐ white letters on an orange background
- ☐ white letters on a yellow background
- ☐ black letters on a yellow background

Question 31 - Practice Test 2

In the event of a tire blowout while driving, you should:

- ☐ Accelerate
- ☐ Brake forcefully
- ☐ Shift to a higher gear
- ☐ Grip the steering wheel tightly

Question 32 - Practice Test 2

Where are car and motorcycle accidents most likely to occur?

- ☐ At roundabouts
- ☐ One-way roads
- ☐ Multi-lane highways
- ☐ At intersections

Question 33 - Practice Test 2

When is it permissible to pass another vehicle?

- ☐ When you are within 100 feet of a railroad crossing
- ☐ When a broken line is present in your lane
- ☐ When a school bus with flashing lights is on the same road
- ☐ On the right shoulder of the highway

Question 34 - Practice Test 2

What strategy should you employ to prevent a collision?

- ☐ Maintain a space cushion
- ☐ Stay on the left side of your lane
- ☐ Switch Lanes frequently
- ☐ Tailgate other vehicles

Question 35 - Practice Test 2

What is the most appropriate method to handle a curve?

- ☐ Slow down before entering the curve
- ☐ Gradually increase your speed before entering the curve
- ☐ Begin turning the vehicle just before the curve and quickly accelerate
- ☐ Stay on your side of the road and drive as far to the left as possible

Question 36 - Practice Test 2

When you approach a roundabout, you should always enter the _____ of the central island.

- ☐ center
- ☐ right
- ☐ corner
- ☐ left

Question 37 - Practice Test 2

What should you do if your brakes fail while you're driving and your vehicle doesn't have antilock brakes (ABS)?

- ☐ Switch into a lower gear
- ☐ Use the parking brake
- ☐ Pump the brake pedal
- ☐ Do all of the above

Question 38 - Practice Test 2

Typically, _____ are diamond-shaped with black letters or symbols on a yellow background.

- ☐ Warning signs
- ☐ Service signs
- ☐ Regulatory signs
- ☐ Destination signs

Question 39 - Practice Test 2

What can be used to guide drivers into specific traffic lanes in work zones during the day and night?

☐ Railroad crossing signals

☐ Large flashing or sequencing arrow panels

☐ Flag persons

☐ Barricades

Question 40 - Practice Test 2

At an intersection, a steady yellow traffic light signifies that you should:

☐ Accelerate to pass the signal before it turns red

☐ Slow down and proceed with caution

☐ Maintain your current speed

☐ Prepare to stop for a red light

PRACTICE TEST 3

We strongly recommend that you go through each question, time yourself, and only review your answers after completing the entire practice test. The answers can be found in the last section of the book.

Total Questions: 40
Correct Answer to pass: 32

Question 1 - Practice Test 3

A vehicle's stopping distance is the total distance it takes to stop, which is equal to:

- ☐ The combined distance of reaction time and following distance
- ☐ The distance traveled while braking
- ☐ The sum of braking distance and following distance
- ☐ The sum of reaction distance and braking distance

Question 2 - Practice Test 3

Vehicles approaching a roundabout should

- ☐ enter the roundabout at a speed of 35 mph
- ☐ enter the roundabout yielding to the traffic already inside
- ☐ enter the roundabout to the left of the central island
- ☐ come to a complete stop and wait for the roundabout traffic to clear

Question 3 - Practice Test 3

A double solid white line _____.

- ☐ indicates that crossing over is prohibited and separates lanes traveling in the same direction
- ☐ indicates that crossing over is permitted and separates lanes traveling in the same direction
- ☐ indicates that crossing over is prohibited and separates opposing lanes
- ☐ indicates that crossing over is permitted and separates opposing lanes

Question 4 - Practice Test 3

When driving on a one-way street with three or more lanes, you should use _____.

- ☐ the center lanes for straight driving and turning
- ☐ the outer lanes for turning and any lane for through travel
- ☐ the outer lanes for straight driving and the center lanes for turning
- ☐ any lane for making turns

Question 5 - Practice Test 3

You shouldn't pass _____.

- ☐ when there is a solid yellow line adjacent to your lane
- ☐ when approaching a hill or curve with limited visibility
- ☐ a school bus ahead displaying flashing red lights and an extended stop arm
- ☐ in any of the situations mentioned above

Question 6 - Practice Test 3

If there are no traffic signals, you should slow down or stop to yield to pedestrians at _____.

- ☐ an intersection
- ☐ an unmarked crosswalk
- ☐ a marked crosswalk
- ☐ all of the above

Question 7 - Practice Test 3

On steep mountain grades, _____ are constructed to safely stop runaway vehicles without causing harm to drivers or passengers.

- ☐ weave lanes
- ☐ escape ramps
- ☐ deceleration lanes
- ☐ acceleration lanes

Question 8 - Practice Test 3

If a driver behind you repeatedly flashes their headlights, you must _____.

- ☐ turn on your low-beam headlights
- ☐ turn on your high-beam headlights
- ☐ move out of the way
- ☐ increase your speed and move forward

Question 9 - Practice Test 3

Which scenario is not advisable for passing another vehicle?

☐   When the road markings are dashed yellow lines

☐   When the road markings are dashed white lines

☐   When the vehicle ahead is moving slower than the safe speed

☐   When you're moving through an intersection

Question 10 - Practice Test 3

Which of the following assertions is incorrect?

☐   Increase your following distance when driving around bicycles

☐   Motorcycles are entitled to the same full lane width as other vehicles

☐   Never drive next to a motorcycle in the same lane

☐   Bicycles and motorcycles move slower and stop slower than expected.

Question 11 - Practice Test 3

If your vehicle's rear wheels begin to skid, what should you do?

☐   Steer the wheel to the left

☐   Steer the wheel in the direction of the skid

☐   Steer the wheel opposite the skid

☐   Steer the wheel to the right

Question 12 - Practice Test 3

When two vehicles approach an intersection from opposite directions at approximately the same time, who has the right-of-way?

☐ The left-turning vehicle must yield to the vehicle going straight or turning right

☐ The vehicle with more passengers should go first

☐ The vehicle on the right must yield to the vehicle on the left

☐ The right-turning vehicle must yield to the left-turning vehicle

Question 13 - Practice Test 3

When entering a roundabout, rotary, or traffic circle, you must yield the right-of-way to:

☐ Pedestrians

☐ Both pedestrians and vehicles already in the circle

☐ Vehicles in the circle

☐ Nobody

Question 14 - Practice Test 3

For improved visibility in fog, rain, or snow, use:

☐ Emergency lights

☐ Low-beam headlights

☐ High-beam headlights

☐ Interior lights

Question 15 - Practice Test 3

You shall not pass a vehicle on the left if:

- ☐ Your lane has a broken white line
- ☐ Your lane has a solid yellow centerline
- ☐ You are far away from a curve
- ☐ Your lane has a broken yellow line

Question 16 - Practice Test 3

_____ enable vehicles to exit expressways.

- ☐ Exit ramps
- ☐ Turnpikes
- ☐ Acceleration lanes
- ☐ Roundabouts

Question 17 - Practice Test 3

To perform a turnaround on a narrow, two-way street, execute:

- ☐ Single-point turn
- ☐ Two-point turn
- ☐ Four-point turn
- ☐ Three-point turn

Question 18 - Practice Test 3

Even ____ alcoholic drink(s) can impact your ability to drive safely.

- ☐ three
- ☐ four
- ☐ one
- ☐ two

Question 19 - Practice Test 3

When another vehicle passes you on the left, you should _____ until the vehicle has safely overtaken you.

- ☐ pull over and stop
- ☐ accelerate and keep to the right
- ☐ slow down and stay to the left
- ☐ slow down and stay centered in your lane

Question 20 - Practice Test 3

When turning right on a multi-lane road, which lane should you typically use?

- ☐ Any lane
- ☐ The leftmost lane
- ☐ A middle lane
- ☐ The rightmost lane

Question 21 - Practice Test 3

When is it prohibited to pass a vehicle on the right?

- ☐ When the vehicle is making a left turn
- ☐ When the vehicle is going straight
- ☐ When the vehicle is making a right turn
- ☐ When the vehicle is on a one-way road with two lanes of traffic

Question 22 - Practice Test 3

In open country at night, which headlights should you use?

☐ High-beam headlights

☐ Parking lights

☐ Low-beam headlights

☐ None of the above

Question 23 - Practice Test 3

Due to their size, tractor-trailers often appear to be _____.

☐ moving faster

☐ moving backward

☐ moving dangerously

☐ moving slower

Question 24 - Practice Test 3

At which locations should you always look both ways?

☐ Railroad crossings

☐ Crosswalks

☐ Intersections

☐ All of the above

Question 25 - Practice Test 3

When is it necessary to signal before passing another vehicle?

- ☐ Always
- ☐ Only if there are vehicles directly behind you
- ☐ If the driver of the vehicle may be unaware of your intention to pass
- ☐ On expressways with more than two lanes

Question 26 - Practice Test 3

When is it appropriate to use your horn?

- ☐ To warn pedestrians or other drivers of potential danger
- ☐ To encourage other drivers to drive faster
- ☐ To inform another driver of their mistake
- ☐ To tell pedestrians to get off the road

Question 27 - Practice Test 3

Which factor does not influence your blood alcohol concentration (BAC)?

- ☐ Time between drinks
- ☐ Your body weight
- ☐ Time since your last drink
- ☐ Type of alcohol consumed

Question 28 - Practice Test 3

Who is responsible for ensuring a child in the vehicle you're driving is properly restrained?

- ☐ The vehicle owner
- ☐ The child
- ☐ Yourself
- ☐ The child's parents

Question 29 - Practice Test 3

If a driver's left arm is extended out the window and bent upward, this indicates they intend to _____.

- ☐ proceed straight
- ☐ slow down or stop
- ☐ turn right
- ☐ turn left

Question 30 - Practice Test 3

A flashing red light signifies _____.

- ☐ caution
- ☐ slowing down
- ☐ the same as a stop sign
- ☐ the same as a yield sign

Question 31 - Practice Test 3

Which areas are most likely to ice over first in freezing temperatures?

- ☐ Bridges and overpasses
- ☐ Residential streets
- ☐ Tunnels
- ☐ Gravel roads

Question 32 - Practice Test 3

When a vehicle merges onto an expressway, who has the right-of-way?

- ☐ The merging vehicle
- ☐ The fastest vehicle
- ☐ Vehicles already on the expressway
- ☐ The slowest vehicle

Question 33 - Practice Test 3

You are the third vehicle to arrive at a four-way stop at different times. Which vehicle has the right-of-way?

- ☐ The vehicle that is not signaling
- ☐ The vehicle turning right
- ☐ The vehicle that arrived first
- ☐ The vehicle to your right

Question 34 - Practice Test 3

You approach a crosswalk with a pedestrian and guide dog attempting to cross the street. What should you do?

☐   Tell the pedestrian it is safe to cross

☐   Stop and turn off your engine

☐   Wait for the pedestrian to cross the street

☐   Honk your horn to indicate it is safe to cross

Question 35 - Practice Test 3

When can you safely merge back in front of a vehicle you just passed?

☐   When the driver honks to let you in

☐   When you see the entire front bumper of the passed vehicle in your rear-view mirror

☐   When you make direct eye contact with the driver in your rearview mirror.

☐   When you can't see the passing vehicle from the window.

Question 36 - Practice Test 3

If you're at a traffic light and a car is speeding toward you from behind, what should you do?

☐   Pull your vehicle forward

☐   Execute a quick U-turn

☐   Maneuver your vehicle to the left

☐   Maneuver your vehicle to the right

Question 37 - Practice Test 3

What are the main aids for a blind person when traveling?

- ☐ A red cane or a trained guide cat
- ☐ A white cane or a wheelchair
- ☐ A red cane or a trained guide dog
- ☐ A white cane or a trained guide dog

Question 38 - Practice Test 3

The distance your vehicle covers from the time you recognize a hazard until you begin to brake is known as _____.

- ☐ the perception distance
- ☐ the stopping distance
- ☐ the reaction distance
- ☐ the braking distance

Question 39 - Practice Test 3

When you're at a railroad crossing that's marked only with a stop sign, when is it safe to proceed?

- ☐ When no train appears to be coming
- ☐ When no pedestrians are coming
- ☐ When no school children are around
- ☐ All of the above

The state of drowsiness or unawareness during freeway driving is known as highway hypnosis. How can you avoid it?

☐ By frequently shifting your gaze

☐ By listening to loud music

☐ By regularly talking on your cell phone

☐ By frequently changing lanes

INTERACTIVE ROAD SIGNS FLASHCARDS

Mastering road signs is a crucial part of your DMV exam preparation. Recognizing and understanding these signs not only helps you pass the test but also ensures you're a safer, more informed driver on the road. To help you solidify your knowledge of road signs, we've created an interactive online tool that you can access from anywhere.

Why Use Flashcards?

Flashcards are a proven study method that can significantly boost your memory retention. By repeatedly testing yourself on the meanings of various road signs, you can quickly identify areas where you need more practice and reinforce the information you already know. They are an effective way to review key concepts in a short amount of time, making them perfect for busy schedules.

Access Our Interactive Flashcards Online

We've developed an awesome online resource where you can practice with digital flashcards designed specifically for road signs. This tool is interactive, easy to use, and accessible from your computer, tablet, or smartphone. Whether you're at home, on your lunch break, or waiting in line, you can take a few minutes to review and test your knowledge.

Access the Flashcards Here:
expert-driving-school.webflow.io

You can also scan the QR code below with your mobile device to access the flashcards instantly:

How to Use the Flashcards

- **Daily Practice:** Set aside a few minutes each day to go through the flashcards. Consistent, short study sessions are more effective than cramming.
- **Test Yourself:** Go through the flashcards in random order to ensure you're not just memorizing the sequence.
- **Track Your Progress:** Note which signs you find challenging and revisit them until you're confident.
- **On-the-Go Learning:** The convenience of accessing these flashcards online means you can fit study sessions into your daily routine, whether you're commuting, on a break, or relaxing at home.

Making the Most of This Resource

The road to passing your DMV exam is made smoother with the right tools, and our interactive flashcards are designed to give you an edge. Combine this resource with the other study materials in this workbook to ensure you're thoroughly prepared.

Remember, understanding road signs is not just about passing the test—it's about becoming a responsible, informed driver. Use these flashcards to build that essential knowledge, and enjoy the confidence that comes with knowing you're ready for the road.

ROAD SIGNS

In the United States, the trend is moving towards using symbols instead of words on road signs for more effective communication. These symbols break down language barriers and facilitate immediate understanding, quickly becoming the global norm for traffic control devices.

It's imperative for all drivers to be well-versed with these traffic sign symbols to ensure the smooth functioning and safety of our transportation networks.

Don't worry, we've got your back. Our resource includes over 50 questions focused on Road Signs to help you master this vital aspect.

Total Questions: 50
Correct Answer to pass: 40

Question 1 - Road Signs

What does this image represent?

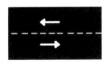

☐ When the way ahead is clear, passing on the left is permitted

☐ Passing on the right is not permitted

☐ Passing is prohibited in both directions

☐ Passing is only permitted during night

Question 2 - Road Signs

What exactly does this road sign mean?

- ☐ A construction zone is ahead

- ☐ There is a parking area ahead

- ☐ There is a forest zone is ahead

- ☐ There's a rest stop ahead

Question 3 - Road Signs

What does this image represent?

- ☐ A child care center

- ☐ T-intersection ahead

- ☐ Playground ahead

- ☐ School zone ahead

Question 4 - Road Signs

What does this sign denote?

- ☐ A side street near a railroad crossing
- ☐ A bridge
- ☐ A Truck service center
- ☐ A pedestrian underpass

Question 5 - Road Signs

This symbol denotes

- ☐ a hospital zone
- ☐ wheelchair accessibility
- ☐ a parking area for the handicapped
- ☐ a pedestrian crosswalk

Question 6 - Road Signs

This orange triangular reflective sign indicates

- ☐ a vehicle that moves in a rapid pace
- ☐ a vehicle transporting hazardous materials
- ☐ a vehicle that moves slowly
- ☐ a truck

Question 7 - Road Signs

Which of these signs points you in the direction of a hospital?

A B C D

- ☐ C
- ☐ B
- ☐ A
- ☐ D

Question 8 - Road Signs

What does this sign indicate?

- ☐ Do not accelerate to 45 mph

- ☐ Drive at a 45-mph speed

- ☐ There is a speed zone is ahead; prepare to slow down to 45 mph

- ☐ Construction zone ahead

Question 9 - Road Signs

Typically, a vertical rectangular traffic sign gives

- ☐ instructions to the driver

- ☐ directions to the driver to come to a halt

- ☐ a warning about the construction work

- ☐ a warning about the road's condition

Question 10 - Road Signs

This symbol denotes

    ☐   a lane for turning left

    ☐   a diversion

    ☐   that the road ahead curves to the left

    ☐   a lane for turning right

Question 11 - Road Signs

This symbol indicates

    ☐   railroad crossing

    ☐   road work

    ☐   a right turn

    ☐   road maintenance

Question 12 - Road Signs

What is the significance of this flashing arrow panel?

☐   The lane ahead of you has been closed

☐   The lane ahead is open for traffic

☐   Flaggers are in front

☐   There are right lane curves ahead

Question 13 - Road Signs

What does this sign indicate?

☐   A divided highway begins ahead

☐   One-way traffic ahead

☐   The divided highway ends ahead

☐   Merging Traffic

Question 14 - Road Signs

What is the meaning of this sign?

☐   When the green arrow is ON, left turns are permitted

☐   When the steady green signal is lit and there are no oncoming vehicles, left turns are permitted

☐   When the green arrow goes out, no left turns are permitted

☐   Left turns are only permitted when the steady green signal is OFF

Question 15 - Road Signs

What exactly does this sign mean?

☐   There is disabled parking ahead.

☐   There is a disabled crossing ahead.

☐   A hospital is on the way.

☐   There is a pedestrian crosswalk ahead.

Question 16 - Road Signs

This warning sign informs drivers that

- ☐   a single-use path crossing ahead

- ☐   there is a school zone ahead

- ☐   it is a bicycle lane

- ☐   a multi-use path crossing is ahead

Question 17 - Road Signs

This symbol indicates that

- ☐   bicyclists should only ride in the lane designated by the sign

- ☐   there is a bikeway crosses the road ahead

- ☐   bicyclists are not allowed to use this lane

- ☐   there is a no-passing zone for bicyclists ahead

Question 18 - Road Signs

If you see this sign while driving in the left lane, what should you do?

    ☐   continue straight

    ☐   merge into the right lane

    ☐   turn left

    ☐   turn right

Question 19 - Road Signs

This warning sign indicates

    ☐   there will be sharp right and left turns

    ☐   the road ahead takes a left turn

    ☐   a winding road

    ☐   that the road ahead bends to the right, then to the left

Question 20 - Road Signs

What does this signal indicate at an intersection?

- ☐ Pedestrians are not allowed to enter the crosswalk
- ☐ Drivers must slow down
- ☐ Pedestrians who are already in the crosswalk may finish their crossing
- ☐ Pedestrians are permitted to enter the crosswalk

Question 21 - Road Signs

What does this symbol indicate?

- ☐ A hospital ahead
- ☐ There is a rest stop ahead
- ☐ High school ahead
- ☐ Handicapped service

Question 22 - Road Signs

This symbol indicates

☐   the exit number 117 is up ahead

☐   next available exit is 117 miles away

☐   to enter the Route 117, take this exit

☐   none of the above

Question 23 - Road Signs

This sign indicates the location of

☐   a gas station

☐   a handicapped service

☐   a rest zone

☐   a hospital zone

Question 24 - Road Signs

What does this sign mean?

☐   Speed limit ahead

☐   Speed restriction on-ramp

☐   Speed advisory at roundabout

☐   An exit speed restriction

Question 25 - Road Signs

What exactly does this sign mean?

☐   Only left turns are permitted

☐   Traffic must merge to the right

☐   Traffic must merge to the left

☐   Only right turns are permitted

Question 26 - Road Signs

What exactly does this sign mean?

- ☐ You shouldn't take a right turn

- ☐ You must not take a left turn

- ☐ This section of the road is closed

- ☐ Do not merge

Question 27 - Road Signs

What exactly does this sign mean?

- ☐ A hospital zone

- ☐ Telephone service available ahead

- ☐ Gas station ahead

- ☐ There will be a rest zone ahead

Question 28 - Road Signs

What exactly does this sign indicate?

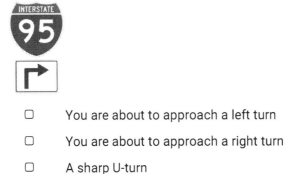

- ☐   You are about to approach a left turn
- ☐   You are about to approach a right turn
- ☐   A sharp U-turn
- ☐   A sharp left turn ahead

Question 29 - Road Signs

What should you do if you see this road sign?

- ☐   Exit the highway at a speed of at least 30 miles per hour
- ☐   Exit the highway at a speed of no more than 30 miles per hour
- ☐   Increase your speed to 30 mph to pass the vehicle in front of you
- ☐   Exit the freeway at a top speed of 60 mph

Question 30 - Road Signs

This pavement markings in this image indicate that

- ☐ It is not allowed to pass
- ☐ You can pass if it is safe
- ☐ Take a detour
- ☐ Make a U turn

Question 31 - Road Signs

What is the meaning of this traffic sign?

- ☐ It is not permissible to pass a vehicle on the left
- ☐ Only left turns are allowed
- ☐ Passing is legal in these directions
- ☐ Only move in the indicated directions

Question 32 - Road Signs

What does this sign mean?

☐   Hospital Zone

☐   You are approaching a A four-way intersection

☐   A side road is ahead

☐   A railroad crossing is ahead

Question 33 - Road Signs

What does this symbol indicate?

☐   Railroad crossing with low ground clearance

☐   Railroad crossing that is closed

☐   Railroad crossing that is being repaired

☐   Byway near a railroad crossing

Question 34 - Road Signs

What does this image mean?

    ☐   A broken white line that forbids passing

    ☐   A broken white line that permits passing

    ☐   An accident occurred

    ☐   The vehicle is making a U-turn

Question 35 - Road Signs

This is an octagonal (eight-sided) figure which indicates

    ☐   a Yield symbol

    ☐   Do Not Enter sign

    ☐   a Stop sign

    ☐   a Construction sign

Question 36 - Road Signs

You can find this orange sign at

- ☐ railroad crossings
- ☐ the intersections that are uncontrolled
- ☐ school zones
- ☐ work zones

Question 37 - Road Signs

What does this sign indicate?

- ☐ A winding road
- ☐ A curve ahead
- ☐ A slippery road
- ☐ A two-way road

Question 38 - Road Signs

What does this sign denote?

☐ A winding road awaits; drivers should follow the signs

☐ A gravel road ahead with sharp curves; drivers must proceed with caution

☐ When the road is wet, it becomes slippery; proceed cautiously

☐ A sharp curve near a hill; vehicles must proceed cautiously

Question 39 - Road Signs

What does this sign indicate?

☐ "Right Lane Ends"

☐ Freeway interchange

☐ Sharp turn on a highway

☐ Beginning of a Divided Highway

Question 40 - Road Signs

What does this sign indicate?

☐   You are not permitted to park on both sides of the sign

☐   You can park on the left side of the sign

☐   Parking is available to the right of the sign

☐   You are not allowed to park to the left of the sign

Question 41 - Road Signs

What does this sign mean?

☐   The divided highway ends

☐   A divided highway begins ahead

☐   There's an underpass ahead

☐   Right lane is closed

Question 42 - Road Signs

This sign means that you are

- ☐ in a wrong lane
- ☐ driving in the wrong direction
- ☐ In the city
- ☐ moving in a bicycle lane

Question 43 - Road Signs

What exactly does this sign mean?

- ☐ Take Route 45
- ☐ The top speed is 45 miles per hour any time
- ☐ The minimum speed limit is 45 miles per hour
- ☐ The maximum speed limit at night is 45 mph

Question 44 - Road Signs

What exactly does this sign indicate?

- ☐ Emergency vehicles may enter the roadway
- ☐ Trucks transporting dangerous materials may enter the road
- ☐ Heavy vehicles may enter the road
- ☐ Farm vehicles may enter the roadway

Question 45 - Road Signs

What should you do if you come across this sign at an intersection?

- ☐ Do not move further
- ☐ Continue right
- ☐ Allow oncoming traffic to pass
- ☐ Before turning right or left, yield the right-of-way or stop

Question 46 - Road Signs

What exactly does this sign indicate?

- ☐   At the sign, all vehicles must make a U-turn
- ☐   U-turns are not permitted for trucks
- ☐   Vehicles are not permitted to make a U-turn at the sign
- ☐   It denotes none of the preceding

Question 47 - Road Signs

What does this sign mean?

- ☐   A side road is ahead
- ☐   A T-intersection is ahead; yield to cross traffic
- ☐   A four-way stop ahead; prepare to yield
- ☐   A tourist information center is ahead

Question 48 - Road Signs

What exactly does this sign mean?

◻   A deer crossing ahead

◻   Cattle crossing ahead

◻   Forest zone

◻   A zoo ahead

Question 49 - Road Signs

What does this sign indicate?

◻   The maximum allowable speed in a school zone

◻   The minimum allowable speed in a school zone

◻   When there are children present in a school zone, this is the maximum allowable speed

◻   When there are children present in a school zone, this is the minimum allowable speed

What does this sign mean?

☐   Parking available

☐   Lodging available

☐   Hospital service available

☐   Handicapped service area available

SIGNS AND SITUATIONS

Presented here is a comprehensive assortment of Signs and Scenarios specifically designed to enhance your understanding of intersections and shared lanes. This collection is not just an assortment of random signs and situations but a carefully curated set of content meant to address all possible scenarios you may encounter on the road.

Total Questions: 25
Correct Answer to pass: 20

Question 1 - Signs & Situations

When you park your vehicle facing downhill next to a curb, in which direction should you turn your front wheels?

☐   Away from the curb

☐   Keep them straight

☐   Toward the curb

☐   It doesn't matter

Question 2 - Signs & Situations

You approach an intersection where the traffic lights are completely out. What should you do?

☐   Yield as you would at a yield sign

☐   Treat the intersection as if there are no signs or signals

☐   Treat the intersection like an all-way stop

☐   Proceed with caution

Question 3 - Signs & Situations

You notice a lane with white diamonds painted on it. What do they imply?

☐ This is a bus only lane

☐ This is a stop lane for emergencies

☐ This lane is now closed

☐ This is a reserved lane

Question 4 - Signs & Situations

At around the same moment, two cars arrive at an intersection. Which of the following statements is correct?

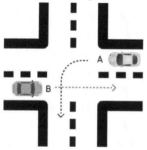

☐ All vehicles turning left must yield to Car B

☐ The drivers must select who will drive first

☐ Car A must yield since it is making a left turn

☐ None of the preceding statements are correct

Question 5 - Signs & Situations

You've parked facing a steep downhill slope. Which of the following actions should you take?

☐   If you have a manual transmission, keep it in reverse

☐   If you have a manual transmission, keep it in first gear

☐   If you have an automatic transmission, keep it in first gear

☐   If you have an automatic transmission, keep it in reverse

Question 6 - Signs & Situations

Three vehicles reach an intersection simultaneously. Who has the right-of-way?

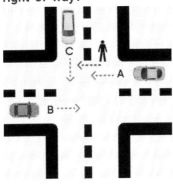

☐   Vehicle B

☐   Vehicle A

☐   The pedestrian

☐   Vehicle C

You notice a yellow "X" light flashing above your lane. What does it imply?

☐ You should exit this lane as soon as possible

☐ This lane is now closed

☐ This lane is clear

☐ This lane is only for turning left

Question 8 - Signs & Situations

You have parked uphill on a steep incline. What should you do?

☐ Set your automatic transmission to first gear

☐ Set your automatic transmission to reverse

☐ Set your manual transmission to first gear

☐ Set your manual transmission to reverse

Question 9 - Signs & Situations

Which of the following takes priority (i.e., should be obeyed above all the others)?

- ☐ A red traffic light
- ☐ A traffic officer
- ☐ A stopped school bus with flashing red lights
- ☐ A warning road sign

Question 10 - Signs & Situations

What should you do when you see a flashing red light?

- ☐ You are not required to stop or yield at a flashing red signal
- ☐ Stop, yield, and then proceed when it is safe to do so
- ☐ Proceed with caution because the traffic signal is out
- ☐ Stop and hold your breath until the light turns green

Question 11 - Signs & Situations

What does the following sign indicate?

- ☐ The minimum speed for this curve is 35 mph
- ☐ The maximum speed for this curve is 35 mph
- ☐ The recommended speed for this curve is 35 mph
- ☐ The curve ahead is 35 degrees

Question 12 - Signs & Situations

You approach an intersection and notice this sign (red octagon shape). What are your options?

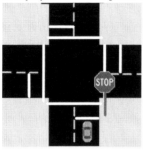

- ☐ Stop completely and yield to traffic before proceeding
- ☐ Stop completely and then proceed
- ☐ Find another route; you cannot proceed through here
- ☐ Slow down and only proceed if the intersection is clear

Question 13 - Signs & Situations

When can you drive in a lane with this sign?

- ☐ When there is at least one passenger
- ☐ Whenever you want
- ☐ When at least two passengers are aboard
- ☐ Never (this is a bus and truck lane)

Question 14 - Signs & Situations

At the same moment, two cars arrive at an uncontrolled intersection (one that is not controlled by signs or signals). Which of the following statements is correct?

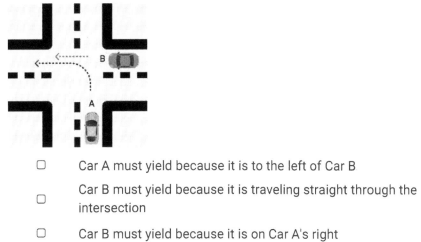

- ☐ Car A must yield because it is to the left of Car B
- ☐ Car B must yield because it is traveling straight through the intersection
- ☐ Car B must yield because it is on Car A's right
- ☐ None of the preceding statements are correct

Question 15 - Signs & Situations

You approach a crossroad with a green light and wish to drive straight through the intersection. Which of the following is correct?

- ☐ You are unable to proceed
- ☐ You are free to continue
- ☐ You may proceed, but you must first yield to any vehicles already present in the crossroads
- ☐ You must temporarily stop and cede before proceeding

Car B enters an intersection intending to turn right on a red light, while Car A has a green light and wants to proceed straight through the intersection. Which statement is accurate?

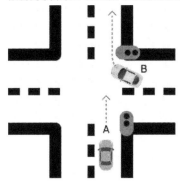

   ☐   Car A should yield to Car B

   ☐   Car A must accelerate to pass Car B

   ☐   Car B should stop and allow Car A to pass

   ☐   None of these options are correct

Before turning left into a driveway, to whom must you yield?

   ☐   Approaching vehicles

   ☐   Pedestrians

   ☐   Both pedestrians and oncoming vehicles

   ☐   No one (you have the right-of-way)

Question 18 - Signs & Situations

Which of the following is correct about driving in rainy conditions?

☐ Roads tend to be most slippery during the first 30 minutes of rain

☐ Avoid using cruise control when driving on wet roads

☐ Turn on your headlights to improve visibility

☐ All of the above

Question 19 - Signs & Situations

You approach an intersection with a STOP sign. Where are you required to stop?

☐ Before entering the intersection

☐ In front of the stop line

☐ Prior to the crosswalk

☐ All of the above options apply

Question 20 - Signs & Situations

You arrive at a crossroads wanting to turn left with a green light. Can you proceed?

☐ Sure, but only if a Left Turn Permitted sign is present

☐ Sure, but first yield to pedestrians and oncoming traffic

☐ No, you may only turn left on a green arrow

☐ Sure, this is a "protected" turn, and you have the right-of-way

You have parked uphill next to a curb. In which direction should you point your front wheels?

- ☐ Away from the curb
- ☐ In any direction
- ☐ Towards the curb
- ☐ Straight

Question 22 - Signs & Situations

You approach an intersection and see the following red sign. What should you do?

- ☐ Slow down and be ready to yield to pedestrians and oncoming traffic
- ☐ Continue at your current speed since the traffic ahead must yield to you
- ☐ Slow down and prepare to yield to traffic ahead, but stopping is not necessary
- ☐ Come to a complete stop, yield to pedestrians and oncoming traffic, and then proceed

The driver is using a hand signal. He/She intends to:

☐ Turn left

☐ Stop

☐ Turn right

☐ Accelerate

Question 24 - Signs & Situations

What action is required when approaching a flashing yellow traffic signal?

☐ Stop, yield, and proceed when safe

☐ Slow down and proceed with caution

☐ Prepare to stop; the signal will soon turn red

☐ Continue straight ahead; turns are not permitted

Question 25 - Signs & Situations

What is the appropriate hand signal to signify that you are slowing or stopping?

☐   Left arm extended straight out to the left

☐   Left arm making a circular motion

☐   Left arm pointing downward

☐   Left arm bent upwards

FINES & LIMITS

This particular segment is tailored to the laws of your State, featuring questions focused on Fines and Limits. It is known to be one of the most challenging sections, often being the stumbling block for many test-takers.

Total Questions: 10
Correct Answer to pass: 8

Question 1 - Fines & Limits

Children aged _____ and under must be secured in a car seat in the vehicle's rear seat.

☐   7

☐   10

☐   8

☐   12

Question 2 - Fines & Limits

How long is your Temporary Alcohol License (TAL) valid?

☐   One year

☐   Three months

☐   Until the hearing results are received by the SCDMV

☐   Until the fine is paid

Question 3 - Fines & Limits

If you get convicted for DUI for the first time, how long will your license be suspended?

- ☐ 60 days
- ☐ 30 days
- ☐ 3 months
- ☐ 6 months

Question 4 - Fines & Limits

At what minimum age can you qualify for a conditional driver's license?

- ☐ 15
- ☐ 15½
- ☐ 16
- ☐ 16½

Question 5 - Fines & Limits

In South Carolina, what's the minimum distance you must maintain from a crosswalk when stopping or parking?

- ☐ 50 feet
- ☐ 20 feet
- ☐ 30 feet
- ☐ 25 feet

Question 6 - Fines & Limits

If an underage driver (under 21 years) is convicted of driving with a BAC above the legal limit, the license will be suspended for how long for a first offense?

- ☐ 2 years
- ☐ 6 months
- ☐ 3 months
- ☐ 1 year

Question 7 - Fines & Limits

How long must you wait to retake your driving test if you fail it once or twice?

- ☐ 2 weeks
- ☐ 60 days
- ☐ 7 days
- ☐ 3 months

Question 8 - Fines & Limits

What's the immediate license suspension duration for a driver under 21 who refuses chemical tests for alcohol or drugs?

- ☐ 6 months
- ☐ 60 days
- ☐ 10 days
- ☐ 30 days

Question 9 - Fines & Limits

When you turn 17 or after you've held a conditional or special restricted license for _____, you'll obtain your full unrestricted license.

☐ 2 years

☐ 6 months

☐ 1 year

☐ 3 months

Question 10 - Fines & Limits

What is the maximum fine for a first-time drug-related driving offense?

☐ $250

☐ $1,000

☐ $500

☐ $2,000

DISTRACTED DRIVING TEST

This section is of paramount importance. It will probe your understanding of contemporary driving distractions, along with the implications of driving under the influence of drugs and medication.

Total Questions: 18
Correct Answer to pass: 15

Question 1 - Distracted Driving

Which of the following statements about cell phones is accurate?

- ☐ It is quicker to make a call while driving
- ☐ The use of a hands-free cell phone while driving is permitted for adults
- ☐ Cell phones can be used while driving for adults
- ☐ If you get a call while you're driving, you should slow down before answering

Question 2 - Distracted Driving

Something happening in the backseat requires your attention while you are driving. What should you do?

- ☐ As you continue to drive, slow down and handle the issue
- ☐ Turn around and cope with the situation, occasionally looking ahead
- ☐ Before addressing the issue, pull over to the side of the road and park your vehicle
- ☐ You should adjust the rearview mirror to see the back seat

Question 3 - Distracted Driving

What should you do before driving if you feel sleepy?

- ☐ Sleep
- ☐ Music-listening
- ☐ consume coffee
- ☐ Exercise

Question 4 - Distracted Driving

What medications, excluding alcohol, can impair one's capacity for safe driving?

- ☐ Prescription drugs
- ☐ Non-prescription medications
- ☐ Medications used to treat migraines, colds, hay fever, various allergies, or to soothe the nerves
- ☐ The entire list above

Question 5 - Distracted Driving

Is it safe to take medications before driving?

- ☐ Only with a valid prescription
- ☐ No
- ☐ Only if the physician states that it won't impair safe driving
- ☐ Only over-the-counter versions

Question 6 - Distracted Driving

It's _____ to text and drive.

- ☐ legal
- ☐ legal if you do not exceed 15 mph
- ☐ legal only when you stop at a STOP sign
- ☐ illegal

Question 7 - Distracted Driving

Talking on a cell phone while driving increases the likelihood of a collision _____.

- ☐ up to four times
- ☐ up to three times
- ☐ by some more amount
- ☐ at least twice

Question 8 - Distracted Driving

Is it legal for teenage drivers to talk on their cell phones while driving?

- ☐ Only when traveling at less than 25 mph
- ☐ Only if you're on a country road
- ☐ Yes, as long as you're cautious
- ☐ It is illegal to use a cell phone while driving

Question 9 - Distracted Driving

To avoid being a distracted driver, you should:

- ☐ smoke, eat, and drink only on straight sections of the road
- ☐ consult maps or use your phone when no other vehicles are around you
- ☐ have all emotionally challenging conversations during your initial hour of driving
- ☐ If possible, switch off your cell phone until you arrive at your destination

Question 10 - Distracted Driving

Fatigue can impact your driving by

- ☐ Compromising your judgment
- ☐ Slowing down your reaction times
- ☐ Reducing your awareness
- ☐ All of the above

Question 11 - Distracted Driving

Potential distractions while driving include:

- ☐ Constantly checking mirrors
- ☐ Checking blind spots
- ☐ Frequently checking the traffic behind you
- ☐ Text messaging and talking on the phone

Question 12 - Distracted Driving

Is it safe to hold something in your lap while driving?

- ☐ Yes, as long as it's not a human or a pet
- ☐ Yes, if it's a small animal
- ☐ Yes, as long as you don't get distracted
- ☐ No way, never

Question 13 - Distracted Driving

To combat highway hypnosis, drowsiness, and fatigue, drivers should _____ to stay awake while driving.

- ☐ Take stimulants
- ☐ Do exercise with their eyes
- ☐ Text message their loved ones
- ☐ Talk on a cell phone

Question 14 - Distracted Driving

Which of the following activities will not negatively affect your driving on the road?

- ☐ Eating
- ☐ Smoking
- ☐ Drinking coffee
- ☐ Listening to the radio

Question 15 - Distracted Driving

A minor driver receives a phone call on their cell phone. He/she should:

- ☐ not carry a cell phone while driving
- ☐ not answer the call
- ☐ use a hands-free cell phone to answer the call
- ☐ answer the call only in an emergency

Question 16 - Distracted Driving

Which of the following actions will NOT help prevent distracted driving?

- ☐ Preprogramming your favorite radio stations
- ☐ Adjusting all your mirrors before starting
- ☐ Pre-loosening the coffee cup lid
- ☐ Preplanning the route

Question 17 - Distracted Driving

Which of the following actions is NOT a safe driving practice?

- ☐ Texting and operating visual screen devices while driving
- ☐ Looking forward and sideways while parking
- ☐ Using side mirrors while you drive
- ☐ Humming to music while you drive

Question 18 - Distracted Driving

Be aware of the following potential distractions or impairments while driving:

- ☐   Alcohol, drugs, and certain medications
- ☐   Adjusting electronic controls and vehicle features
- ☐   Listening to loud music, using devices such as cell phones, GPS, and intercoms
- ☐   All of the above mentioned

DRINKING AND DRIVING TEST

This segment delves into the repercussions of driving under the influence of alcohol. It's essential to grasp the restrictions associated with alcohol consumption and its impact on your physical condition while driving.

Total Questions: 20
Correct Answer to pass: 16

Question 1 - Drinking and Driving

If you're unable to drive due to excessive alcohol consumption, what should you do?

☐ Have a designated driver take you home

☐ Call 911 for assistance in driving

☐ Drink coffee to stay awake while driving

☐ Take drugs to counteract the effects of alcohol before driving

Question 2 - Drinking and Driving

What can help an intoxicated person sober up?

☐ Time

☐ A cup of coffee

☐ Cold and fresh air

☐ All of the above

Question 3 - Drinking and Driving

What are the potential penalties for being convicted of driving under the influence of alcohol or drugs?

- ☐ License suspension
- ☐ Substantial fines and higher insurance rates
- ☐ Community service
- ☐ Any or all of the above

Question 4 - Drinking and Driving

Which is NOT a consequence of consuming alcohol?

- ☐ Increased alertness
- ☐ Slow reactions
- ☐ Impaired judgment
- ☐ Hindered vision

Question 5 - Drinking and Driving

Which of the following beverages has a standard 1.5-ounce amount of alcohol?

- ☐ A 5-ounce glass of wine
- ☐ One can of beer
- ☐ One shot of 80-proof liquor
- ☐ Each of the above

Question 6 - Drinking and Driving

Why is consuming alcohol and driving at night particularly dangerous?

- ☐ Alcohol impairs judgment more at night
- ☐ There's a higher chance of encountering drunk drivers
- ☐ Vision is already restricted
- ☐ Roads are busier at night

Question 7 - Drinking and Driving

Which factor does not impact blood alcohol concentration?

- ☐ Time during which alcohol was consumed
- ☐ Body weight
- ☐ Time since the last drink
- ☐ Alcohol type

Question 8 - Drinking and Driving

How does alcohol consumption impact driving ability?

- ☐ Reduces driving skills
- ☐ Negatively affects depth perception
- ☐ Slows down reflexes
- ☐ All of the above

Question 9 - Drinking and Driving

Which of the following actions will result in the mandatory suspension of a minor's license?

- ☐ Driving when impaired by drugs
- ☐ Transporting an open beer container
- ☐ Transporting an open liquor container
- ☐ Any or all of the preceding

Question 10 - Drinking and Driving

What is the leading cause of death for Americans aged 16 to 24?

- ☐ Kidney problems
- ☐ Drunk driving
- ☐ Drug overdose
- ☐ Cancer

Question 11 - Drinking and Driving

It is prohibited to have open containers of alcohol in a vehicle in which of the following places?

- ☐ The driver's seat
- ☐ The console
- ☐ beneath the seat
- ☐ In all of the preceding

Question 12 - Drinking and Driving

Alcohol can have an impact on your:

- ☐ Reaction time
- ☐ Judgment
- ☐ Concentration
- ☐ All of the answers given above are correct.

Question 13 - Drinking and Driving

Drinking and driving can _____.

- ☐ Impair your reflexes
- ☐ Reduce physical control over a vehicle
- ☐ Decrease a driver's awareness of road hazards
- ☐ All of the above

Question 14 - Drinking and Driving

Which of the following statements about drivers under the age of twenty-one is correct?

- ☐ They are not permitted to purchase, drink, or possess alcohol
- ☐ They are permitted to consume limited amounts of alcohol, but not while driving
- ☐ They can buy alcohol but not consume it. They can have trace levels of alcohol in their blood while driving
- ☐ They are allowed to have trace amounts of alcohol in their blood while driving

Question 15 - Drinking and Driving

After consuming a significant amount of alcohol, you can ensure you will not be driving under the influence by:

☐ Waiting a day or two

☐ Drinking only beer or wine, not hard liquor

☐ Waiting at least an hour

☐ Waiting at least 30 minutes

Question 16 - Drinking and Driving

Which of the following regions does NOT allow open containers of alcohol?

☐ Passenger areas of standard passenger cars

☐ Limousine passenger compartments

☐ In a passenger car's trunk

☐ Motorhome residential areas

Question 17 - Drinking and Driving

Which of the following is an acceptable substitute for drinking and driving?

☐ Public transportation

☐ A designated driver

☐ A taxi

☐ All of the preceding

Question 18 - Drinking and Driving

A driver who has consumed alcohol is more likely to _____.

☐ fail to dim headlights for oncoming traffic

☐ drive too fast or too slowly

☐ change lanes frequently

☐ do all of the preceding tasks

Question 19 - Drinking and Driving

As a driver's blood alcohol concentration (BAC) increases, which of the following occurs?

☐ Alcohol impairs coordination and muscle control

☐ Alcohol has a growing impact on the brain of the drinker

☐ The first processes to be impacted are self-control and judgment

☐ All of the aforementioned

Question 20 - Drinking and Driving

How many standard servings of alcohol can an adult safely consume before driving?

☐ It varies depending on the individual.

☐ 2

☐ 1

☐ 3

MOCK TEST

This is the final part of the book. Sit back, relax, and focus. This practice test contains the same number of questions as the official DMV exam. Good luck! If you find yourself still making too many mistakes, we strongly recommend downloading the additional 200 questions in the resource section to further prepare for the exam!

Total Questions: 30
Correct Answer to pass: 24

Question 1 - Mock Exam

What is the correct procedure for making turns?

☐ Always initiate the turn from the far-right lane

☐ Always initiate the turn from the far-left lane

☐ Begin your turn from the lane that is furthest from your intended direction

☐ Begin your turn from the lane that is nearest to your intended direction.

Question 2 - Mock Exam

Before crossing an intersection, what should you look out for?

☐ Vehicles coming from the right

☐ Vehicles coming from the left

☐ Pedestrians crossing

☐ All of the above

Question 3 - Mock Exam

When turning left at a controlled intersection (one with traffic signs or lights), whom should you yield to?

- ☐ Vehicles that are making a right turn
- ☐ Vehicles that are to your right
- ☐ Oncoming traffic
- ☐ Vehicles that are behind you

Question 4 - Mock Exam

If you encounter a _____ sign in your lane, it implies you are driving in the wrong direction.

- ☐ One Way
- ☐ Do Not Enter
- ☐ Road Closed
- ☐ Detour

Question 5 - Mock Exam

In a multilane roundabout, which lane should you use if you plan to exit before reaching the halfway point?

- ☐ The left lane
- ☐ The middle lane
- ☐ The right lane
- ☐ None of the above

Question 6 - Mock Exam

A _____ shows the roadway's outer edge and can only be crossed when moving to or from the shoulder.

- ☐ solid yellow line
- ☐ dashed white line
- ☐ solid white line
- ☐ dashed yellow line

Question 7 - Mock Exam

Which situation is NOT advisable for overtaking another vehicle?

- ☐ When road markings are dashed white lines
- ☐ When road markings are dashed yellow lines
- ☐ When you're traversing an intersection
- ☐ When the car in front of you is moving slower than the safe speed

Question 8 - Mock Exam

How soon must you inform the SCDMV after a name or address change?

- ☐ Within 15 days
- ☐ Within 10 days
- ☐ Within 7 days
- ☐ Within 30 days

Question 9 - Mock Exam

Why are warning signs installed along roadways?

- ☐ To supply information about directions, distances, and amenities
- ☐ To manage and regulate the flow of traffic
- ☐ To highlight landmarks and geographical data
- ☐ To alert drivers to possible hazards ahead

Question 10 - Mock Exam

What is permitted with a route-restricted driver's license?

- ☐ Going to school
- ☐ Attending ADSAP courses
- ☐ Commuting to work
- ☐ All of the above

Question 11 - Mock Exam

What behaviors are indicative of road rage?

- ☐ Following too closely
- ☐ Forcing another vehicle off the road
- ☐ Excessive horn honking
- ☐ All of the above

Question 12 - Mock Exam

What should you do to signal when you are slowing down or stopping?

- ☐ Use a hand signal to notify the trailing driver
- ☐ Use brake lights to notify the trailing driver
- ☐ Use both hand signal and brake lights
- ☐ Use either hand signal or brake lights

Question 13 - Mock Exam

How far ahead should you look when driving in city traffic?

- ☐ Two blocks ahead
- ☐ Three blocks ahead
- ☐ Four blocks ahead
- ☐ One block ahead

Question 14 - Mock Exam

In South Carolina, what does a yellow-painted curb signify?

- ☐ Parking briefly to load or unload is allowed
- ☐ You may stop briefly to make a quick turn
- ☐ You can stop until it's safe to pass
- ☐ Parking is not permitted

Question 15 - Mock Exam

What type of accident is most common on interstate highways?

- ☐ Head-on collisions
- ☐ Collisions involving trucks
- ☐ Rear-end collisions
- ☐ Side-impact collisions

When two cars meet on a narrow mountain road and neither can pass, who has the right-of-way?

- ☐ The vehicle moving uphill
- ☐ The vehicle moving downhill
- ☐ The vehicle that arrived first
- ☐ Neither vehicle

If a police officer stops you for a traffic violation, what documents must you show?

- ☐ Insurance proof
- ☐ Driver's license
- ☐ Vehicle registration
- ☐ All of the above

What does a steady red arrow signal indicate?

- ☐ You may safely turn in the arrow's direction
- ☐ You must stop and can't proceed in the arrow's direction
- ☐ Prepare to stop and yield to oncoming traffic before turning
- ☐ Complete a full stop and then proceed when safe

Question 19 - Mock Exam

What can help you become sober after consuming alcohol?

- ☐ Eating food
- ☐ Drinking coffee
- ☐ The passage of time
- ☐ Taking a cold shower

Question 20 - Mock Exam

When parallel parking next to a curb, your vehicle must be within how many inches of the curb?

- ☐ 20 inches
- ☐ 18 inches
- ☐ 12 inches
- ☐ 40 inches

Question 21 - Mock Exam

When should you adjust your seat and mirrors?

- ☐ Before entering the vehicle
- ☐ At the first crossroads
- ☐ After you've started driving
- ☐ Prior to initiating your drive

Question 22 - Mock Exam

What is typical of speed limits in work zones?

- ☐ No speed limits exist
- ☐ Speed limits are increased
- ☐ A 45-mph speed limit is imposed
- ☐ Speed limits are decreased

Question 23 - Mock Exam

What should you do if your accelerator gets stuck?

- ☐ Shift into neutral
- ☐ Slam on the brakes
- ☐ Drive until you're out of gas
- ☐ Dial 911 immediately

Question 24 - Mock Exam

When you arrive at an intersection, which direction should you look first and why?

- ☐ Right; vehicles from the right are nearer
- ☐ Right; vehicles from the right have the right-of-way
- ☐ Left; vehicles from the left have the right-of-way
- ☐ Left; vehicles from the left are closer

Question 25 - Mock Exam

If you need to make an emergency stop, what should you do?

- ☐ Flash your headlights
- ☐ Lift your vehicle's hood
- ☐ Stay inside the car
- ☐ Keep the engine running

Question 26 - Mock Exam

What should you not rely on solely when reversing your vehicle?

- ☐ Using your mirrors
- ☐ The brake's effectiveness
- ☐ Looking out the back window
- ☐ Checking over your shoulder

Question 27 - Mock Exam

What should you do when making a right turn?

- ☐ Stick close to the curb
- ☐ Always stop fully before turning
- ☐ Avoid the lane closest to the curb
- ☐ Make a wide turn to avoid the curb

Question 28 - Mock Exam

When can you cross two solid yellow lines?

- ☐ When making a left turn
- ☐ When initiating a right turn
- ☐ While overtaking the vehicle in front of you
- ☐ When moving for an emergency vehicle

Under which violations could you qualify for a Temporary Alcohol License (TAL)?

☐ Implied Consent

☐ Blood Alcohol Concentration (BAC) of 0.15%

☐ Both the above

☐ Either of the above

Question 30 - Mock Exam

If your vehicle breaks down and you can't get it fully off the road, where should you stop?

☐ In a ditch

☐ At the middle of a curb

☐ On the crest of a hill

☐ Where your vehicle is visible from behind

A MESSAGE FROM THE DRIVING SCHOOL

As we wrap up this workbook, we just wanted to say a big thank you! We're so glad you chose us to be a part of your journey towards mastering the art of driving. It's been an absolute pleasure helping you get closer to acing that DMV exam.

We genuinely care about your success and satisfaction, and we're always looking for ways to make our resources better. That's where you come in - we'd love to hear your thoughts about this workbook.

Your feedback is like gold dust to us. It not only helps us improve, but it also guides future learners who are just starting out on their driving journey. So, if you have a spare moment and liked this book, would you mind sharing your experience with this workbook?

Leaving a review is easy as pie. Just head over to where you bought the book and let us know what you think. For the paperback version, you can find a QR code on the back cover that will take you directly to the review page. Every single word you share matters to us, and we're really excited to hear about your learning journey. If you have found any issue or you have suggestions on how to improve this book, feel free to write to us at info@infiniteinkpress.org.

Once again, a big thank you for picking our workbook. We're cheering you on and wishing you all the best as you hit the road and put all that learning into action. Safe driving and take care!

Thank you so much,

Expert Driving School

ANSWER SHEET

PRACTICE TEST 1

Question 1 - Practice Test 1

(C) In the absence of a functional traffic signal, South Carolina law mandates that drivers must yield to pedestrians crossing the road, whether in a marked or unmarked crosswalk. You should wait until the pedestrian has completely crossed at least your half of the road before proceeding.

Question 2 - Practice Test 1

(C) If you've missed a turn at a intersection, continue to the next intersection and make the necessary turns to return to your intended route.

Question 3 - Practice Test 1

(B) When a U-turn isn't possible due to limited space, consider executing a three-point turn. This also results in your car facing the opposite direction and should only be attempted on narrow streets with low traffic and clear visibility, and where it is legally permitted.

Question 4 - Practice Test 1

(D) At intersections, adhere to the "left-right-left" rule for checking traffic. First, look to your left where oncoming vehicles are nearest to you, then look to your right. Finally, check to your left once more before moving, as you may have missed a vehicle the first time you looked.

Question 5 - Practice Test 1

(B) The distance required to brake increases exponentially with speed. Doubling your speed will quadruple your braking distance and tripling your speed will make your braking distance nine times longer.

Question 6 - Practice Test 1

(A) Head restraints are engineered to minimize neck injuries in rear-end collisions. Adjust the headrest so that it would make contact with the back of your head should an accident occur.

Question 7 - Practice Test 1

(A) Double solid yellow lines in the middle of the road signify that overtaking is not allowed from either direction.

Question 8 - Practice Test 1

(B) If you miss an exit or take the wrong one in South Carolina, do not reverse on the highway, as this is both dangerous and illegal. Also, avoid using median crossovers, which are reserved for authorized vehicles like emergency and maintenance units.

Question 9 - Practice Test 1

(C) Roundabouts are one-way, circular intersections where vehicles circulate counterclockwise around a central island. To enter, turn right and yield to oncoming traffic already in the circle.

Question 10 - Practice Test 1

(B) If another vehicle is overtaking you, maintain your lane and speed to allow the driver to pass you securely.

Question 11 - Practice Test 1

(D) Mile markers, or mileposts, are positioned every 0.2 miles along the roadside to help drivers know their location. They serve navigational and emergency purposes and are found on the road's outer shoulder.

Question 12 - Practice Test 1

(A) An interchange is a junction designed for roads to intersect without obstructing each other's flow. They are connected by ramps that let you switch from one road to another seamlessly. Types of interchanges include diamond, cloverleaf, and folded diamond designs, among others.

Question 13 - Practice Test 1

(D) On multi-lane highways, try not to drive beside other vehicles to avoid the risk of someone invading your lane or making an abrupt lane change into you.

Question 14 - Practice Test 1

(C) When you approach or pass through a work zone, watch what other drivers are doing and do not weave from lane to lane. Gradually brake to give trailing vehicles enough time to adjust their speed and try to maintain the general speed of traffic.

Question 15 - Practice Test 1

(C) Upon seeing a yield sign in your lane, slow down and stop if needed to allow pedestrians and vehicles on the intersecting road to pass.

Question 16 - Practice Test 1

(B) If you collide with a parked car when the owner isn't present, leave a note containing your contact details and the vehicle owner's name. Attach the note securely to the parked car. If the damage looks like it's over $1,000, file an accident report with the SCDMV.

Question 17 - Practice Test 1

(B) When exiting a high-speed, two-lane road, avoid abrupt deceleration to prevent being rear-ended. Signal your intent with turn signals, and gradually decrease your speed.

Question 18 - Practice Test 1

(B) During a turn, a vehicle's rear wheels trace a shorter arc compared to its front wheels. This discrepancy is more pronounced for longer vehicles like tractor-trailers. Be cautious when such vehicles move left, as they might actually be preparing to turn right. Check their indicators for confirmation.

Question 19 - Practice Test 1

(B) If you suffer a tire blowout, keep a firm grip on the steering wheel and continue in a straight line. Gradually lift your foot off the gas pedal. Only apply the brakes gently after regaining control. Move off the road to a safe location as soon as possible.

Question 20 - Practice Test 1

(D) When no traffic control signals are present, slow down or stop to allow pedestrians to cross at intersections or any marked or unmarked crosswalks. According to South Carolina law, you should wait until the pedestrian has fully crossed at least your part of the road.

Question 21 - Practice Test 1

(B) If your engine quits while driving around a bend, grab the steering wheel with both hands and steer to the right side of the road. (If your vehicle has power steering, a loss of engine power will result in a loss of power assist, requiring you to apply greater force to the steering wheel.) Bring your vehicle to a complete stop. (If your vehicle has power brakes, a lack of engine power will result in a loss of power assist, requiring you to push the brake pedal extra hard.) Shift the transmission into park (for automatic transmissions) or neutral (for manual transmissions) and try to restart the engine.

Question 22 - Practice Test 1

(A) You are not allowed to drive over a median or barrier that separates two lanes of a highway into two different routes unless it is an authorized crossover.

Question 23 - Practice Test 1

(D) Driving smoothly enables you to maintain a greater safety buffer between you and other motorists. It also aids in gas savings. The middle lanes offer the most consistently smooth traffic flow when there are three or more lanes traveling in one direction. Drivers that want to travel more quickly, pass, or make a left turn should use the left lane. Use the right lane for slower moving vehicles and those making a right turn.

Question 24 - Practice Test 1

(D) You don't have as much traction on gravel or dirt roads as you do on concrete or asphalt. You might skid as you turn and stopping will take significantly longer. Better slow down.

Question 25 - Practice Test 1

(A) Avoid loitering in a No-Zone! Large zones around trucks and other large vehicles are known as "No-Zones," whereby cars may enter blind spots or approach so closely as to impair the truck

driver's ability to stop or maneuver safely. No-Zones significantly raise the risk of a collision.

Question 26 - Practice Test 1

(D) You should look in the front, sides, and rear before starting to back up, and you should keep looking in the rear as you do so. Be wary of your mirrors because they have blind zones.

Question 27 - Practice Test 1

(D) A broken line next to your lane means you can cross it for passing or changing lanes if it's safe.

Question 28 - Practice Test 1

(A) Angle parking is frequently seen in parking lots, malls, and on broad avenues. Keep an eye out for pedestrians and oncoming traffic before and after you pull into an angle parking place and avoid parking too near to other cars.

Question 29 - Practice Test 1

(A) Passing must always be done safely. Wait until you can see both headlights of the passed vehicle in your rearview mirror before attempting to move back into your original lane. Next, activate your turn signal, scan your blind spots, and move back into the original lane.

Question 30 - Practice Test 1

(B) Tailgating, or following too closely, is a leading cause of rear-end accidents on highways. Maintain a safe distance from the vehicle ahead.

Question 31 - Practice Test 1

(D) Pulling your car off the road should be your first action if you are one of the first people on the scene of a collision. Move injured people only if there is a fire hazard. Notify emergency personnel and stay out of the lanes of traffic. Those who have already stopped should signal oncoming traffic.

Question 32 - Practice Test 1

(A) To lessen the chance of skidding, slow down before entering the curve so you don't need to brake while in it.

Question 33 - Practice Test 1

(D) The brakes will fade (lose their efficacy) if you continually applying the brakes to reduce your speed while descending a steep slope. Instead, let off the gas and downshift (even if your transmission is automatic). This will provide engine braking, which will cause the car to slow down. The engine braking effect increases with lower gearing. Only when engine braking is insufficient or you need to stop should you apply the brakes.

Question 34 - Practice Test 1

(C) Keep the driving wheel straight as you turn your head to examine your blind zones. (People naturally turn their arms in the same direction that they tilt their heads.)

Question 35 - Practice Test 1

(C) The SCDMV will send you a letter advising you to drive more cautiously if you are 15 or 16 years old and have two points and/or four points on your driving record. Your driving privileges will be suspended for at least three months if you receive 12 or more points.

Question 36 - Practice Test 1

(D) For passing on a multi-lane road, use the middle or left lanes.

Question 37 - Practice Test 1

(B) Uneven tires or low pressure can result in faster tire wear, reduced fuel efficiency, and make your vehicle harder to control and stop.

Question 38 - Practice Test 1

(D) Total stopping distance is the sum of your perception distance (the amount of time it takes for your brain to process a hazard after you see it), reaction distance (the amount of time it takes for your foot to begin braking after your brain commands it to do so), and braking distance (the amount of additional distance the vehicle travels after you apply the brakes).

Question 39 - Practice Test 1

(D) Before reaching a hill's crest or entering a curve, reduce speed, move to the road's right side, and watch for oncoming traffic.

Question 40 - Practice Test 1

(D) Total stopping distance is made up of your perception distance (the distance your car travels between the time your eyes first spot a hazard and the time your brain processes it), reaction distance (the distance your car travels between the time your brain commands your foot to start braking and the actual braking itself), and braking distance (the distance the car travels after you apply the brakes).

PRACTICE TEST 2

Question 1 - Practice Test 2

(D) When heated, oil within the asphalt rises to the surface, and rainwater can further dislodge these oil deposits. This creates a more slippery surface until additional rainfall washes the oil away.

Question 2 - Practice Test 2

(B) When a vehicle's turn signals are not functioning, the driver must use hand and arm signals. A right turn is indicated by a 90-degree upward-pointing arm, a left turn is shown by an extended leftward arm, and slowing down or stopping is signaled by a 90-degree downward-pointing arm.

Question 3 - Practice Test 2

(D) If your engine stops working mid-curve, use both hands to firmly steer to the right side of the road. Losing engine power will mean losing power-assisted steering and brakes, necessitating more force on the steering wheel and brake pedal. Once stopped, shift to park (automatic transmission) or neutral (manual transmission) and attempt to restart the engine.

Question 4 - Practice Test 2

(C) Safety belts are known to save lives, including those in the rear seats. In an accident, they can significantly reduce the risk of serious injuries.

Question 5 - Practice Test 2

(B) Tailgating, or following too closely, is a primary reason for rear-end collisions on highways. It's crucial to keep a safe distance from the vehicle ahead.

Question 6 - Practice Test 2

(C) To prevent a head-on collision, steer right towards the shoulder or curb. Don't steer left; the other driver might attempt to correct their course. Be ready to entirely leave the roadway to the right if needed.

Question 7 - Practice Test 2

(C) Vehicles in a roundabout move around a central island in a counterclockwise direction. The design of these intersections is intended to reduce both the number and severity of collisions.

Question 8 - Practice Test 2

(D) When you're getting ready to leave a parallel parking spot, it's important to do all of the above. Check your mirrors, look over your shoulder, and signal your intention to move. Wait until the road is clear before pulling into traffic and stay in the nearest lane until it's safe to switch lanes.

Question 9 - Practice Test 2

(B) If your vehicle gets stuck on railroad tracks and a train is coming, avoid trying to free the vehicle. Instead, ensure everyone exits the vehicle and swiftly moves at a 45-degree angle away from the tracks in the direction the train is coming. This way, you and any passengers will not be hit by debris if the car is struck. Contact 911 or call the number displayed on the railroad crossing sign.

Question 10 - Practice Test 2

(A) When double solid lines are adjacent to your lane, passing or changing lanes is prohibited.

Question 11 - Practice Test 2

(D) When driving on wet pavement at speeds up to 35 mph, modern tires generally disperse water to maintain road contact. However, at higher speeds in deep water, tire channeling becomes less effective, causing the tires to glide on the water like water skis. This phenomenon is called "hydroplaning." At 50 mph or above, hydroplaning can lead to a complete loss of braking and steering control. To avoid hydroplaning, reduce your speed.

Question 12 - Practice Test 2

(C) When two vehicles meet on a steep mountain road where neither can pass, the vehicle descending must yield the right-of-way by reversing until the vehicle ascending can pass. The vehicle facing downhill has more control when backing up.

Question 13 - Practice Test 2

(C) You can avoid sudden, panic stops by identifying potential hazards well in advance and planning how to handle them. Abrupt stopping is dangerous and is usually indicative of a driver who is not paying attention. If you stop suddenly, you risk being rear-ended by the vehicle behind you or skidding and losing control of your vehicle.

Question 14 - Practice Test 2

(C) If your gas pedal is stuck, DON'T PANIC. Try to lift the gas pedal with your foot. If that doesn't work, switch your vehicle to neutral to disengage power to the drive wheels. Then, apply brakes to slow down and steer your vehicle off the road.

Question 15 - Practice Test 2

(B) Continually applying brakes to control your speed while descending a steep hill can cause brake fade, which reduces their effectiveness. Instead, release the gas pedal and shift into a lower gear (even with an automatic transmission). This will create a braking effect known as engine braking to slow down the vehicle. Apply brakes only when engine braking is insufficient or you want to stop. You should never coast downhill in neutral or (for manual transmissions) with the clutch depressed.

Question 16 - Practice Test 2

(C) On gravel or dirt roads, your vehicle doesn't have as much traction as on concrete or asphalt roads. This will extend your stopping distance, and you may skid when you turn. Therefore, slow down.

Question 17 - Practice Test 2

(C) If you're being tailgated, shift to the right lane and decrease your speed to encourage the tailgater to pass you on your left. Do not accelerate in an attempt to placate or outrun the tailgater. No speed is too fast for some tailgaters.

Question 18 - Practice Test 2

(D) Increasing your speed amplifies your braking distance as the square of the speed increases. If you double your speed, your braking distance becomes not twice as long but four times as long. If you triple your speed, your braking distance becomes nine times as long.

Question 19 - Practice Test 2

(A) Defensive driving, as defined by the National Safety Council, is "driving to save lives, time, and money, in spite of the conditions around you and the actions of others." It involves anticipating potentially dangerous situations in advance, including road conditions and errors made by other drivers, and planning how to respond to these situations. This includes constant awareness of driving conditions, planning ahead, anticipating hazards, and taking appropriate actions to prevent collisions with obstacles or other vehicles.

Question 20 - Practice Test 2

(D) When passing, maintain a safe distance from the other vehicle. Don't attempt to return to your original lane until you can see the entire front of the vehicle you just overtook in your rear-view mirror. Then, activate your turn signal, check your blind spots, and smoothly move back into the original lane.

Question 21 - Practice Test 2

(D) On highways with three or more lanes in the same direction, the middle lanes often provide the smoothest traffic flow. The left lane is primarily for drivers who wish to go faster, overtake other vehicles, or make a left turn. Slower vehicles and those intending to turn right should use the right lane.

Question 22 - Practice Test 2

(A) Your chances of survival in a car crash increase when you use both the lap and shoulder belts. The lap belt should be adjusted to fit snugly across the hips or upper thighs, never across the abdomen or soft part of the stomach. The shoulder belt should fit snugly across the chest and midpoint of the shoulder.

Question 23 - Practice Test 2

(A) When changing lanes, preparing to overtake another vehicle, or merging into traffic, signal your intentions and check for any traffic that may be passing you. Start by using your mirrors. Once your mirrors indicate it's safe to proceed, check your vehicle's blind spots by looking over your shoulder in the direction you plan to move.

Question 24 - Practice Test 2

(D) For smoother and safer driving, keep a safe distance between you and other drivers and save gas. On roadways with three or more lanes going in the same direction, the middle lanes usually offer the smoothest flow of traffic. The left lane is primarily for drivers who want to go faster, overtake, or turn left. Slower vehicles and those intending to turn right should use the right lane.

Question 25 - Practice Test 2

(A) Backing up can be dangerous because it can be difficult to see everything behind your vehicle, and other drivers typically don't expect a vehicle to be moving backward towards them. It's best to avoid backing into traffic whenever possible. However, when entering a driveway or a parallel parking space, you may need to back into it unless signs prohibit doing so. This way, when you pull out, you'll be moving forward.

Question 26 - Practice Test 2

(A) Motorcycles, like all other vehicles, need a full lane's width to maneuver safely. Therefore, you should never drive alongside a motorcycle in the same lane, even if the lane is wide and the motorcyclist is riding to one side. This is to ensure the safety of both the motorcyclist and yourself.

Question 27 - Practice Test 2

(A) Vertical rectangular signs that have black letters on a white background are typically regulatory signs. These include speed limit signs and lane usage signs, among others.

Question 28 - Practice Test 2

(D) To make a right turn, look left and right, yield the right-of-way, and hand-over-hand turn the steering wheel to complete the turn in the lane next to the curb.

Question 29 - Practice Test 2

(D) A flashing yellow traffic signal implies that you should slow down and proceed with caution. These lights are typically located at comparatively hazardous spots.

Question 30 - Practice Test 2

(A) Signs indicating construction, maintenance, or emergency operations are usually diamond-shaped or rectangular with black symbols or letters on an orange background. They serve to alert drivers that people are working in or near the roadway.

Question 31 - Practice Test 2

(D) If you experience a sudden tire blowout, firmly hold the steering wheel and gradually ease off the gas pedal. Apply gentle braking only after regaining control of your vehicle.

Question 32 - Practice Test 2

(D) Intersections are the locations where car and motorcycle accidents are most frequently encountered. This often occurs when a car driver overlooks the presence of a motorcycle and turns into its path.

Question 33 - Practice Test 2

(B) Passing is permitted when a broken line, either white or yellow, is adjacent to your lane.

Question 34 - Practice Test 2

(A) Creating a buffer of space around your vehicle, in all directions, is an effective method to prevent collisions.

Question 35 - Practice Test 2

(A) Decreasing your speed before entering a curve is advisable as braking during a curve can lead to skidding.

Question 36 - Practice Test 2

(B) When approaching a roundabout, vehicles must yield to traffic circulating the roundabout and should always enter to the right of the central island.

Question 37 - Practice Test 2

(D) In case of brake failure, remain calm. Try pumping the brake pedal unless your vehicle has ABS, which may restore some brake fluid pressure. If your vehicle has ABS, depress the brake pedal firmly. Additionally, downshift to a lower gear to use engine braking, and apply the parking brake gradually, being ready to release it to prevent skidding. As a last resort, try to slow down by brushing against something, such as a guard rail, rubbing your wheels against a curb, or driving onto a grassy area. Avoid a head-on collision at all costs as these are often fatal.

Question 38 - Practice Test 2

(A) Warning signs are generally diamond-shaped with black letters or symbols on a yellow background.

Question 39 - Practice Test 2

(B) During both day and night, large flashing or sequencing arrow panels can be used in work zones to guide drivers into specific traffic lanes and to notify them of road or street closures ahead.

Question 40 - Practice Test 2

(D) A steady yellow traffic light serves as a warning that the light will soon turn red. Prepare to stop for a red light, but avoid suddenly stopping if there's a vehicle close behind you to prevent a rear-end collision. If stopping safely isn't possible, cautiously proceed through the intersection.

PRACTICE TEST 3

Question 1 - Practice Test 3

(D) A vehicle's stopping distance is the total distance it takes to come to a complete stop. This distance is the sum of two components: the reaction distance (the distance the vehicle travels while the driver reacts and begins to apply the brakes) and the braking distance (the distance the vehicle travels while the brakes are slowing it down). Various factors, such as the vehicle's speed, the driver's alertness, and the condition of the brakes, can influence the overall stopping distance.

Question 2 - Practice Test 3

(B) When approaching a roundabout, drivers must yield the right-of-way to the traffic that is already circulating inside the roundabout. It is important to enter the roundabout on the right (counterclockwise) side, maintaining an appropriate speed.

Question 3 - Practice Test 3

(A) A double solid white line signifies that crossing over the line is prohibited and serves as a separator for lanes traveling in the same direction. Such lines are commonly used on highways to separate high-occupancy vehicle (HOV) lanes from other lanes in the same direction.

Question 4 - Practice Test 3

(B) On a one-way street with three or more lanes, drivers should use the outer lanes for turning and any lane for straight driving unless signs or road markings indicate otherwise.

Question 5 - Practice Test 3

(D) Passing is prohibited when there is a solid yellow line adjacent to your lane. It is also forbidden to pass a school bus that has activated its flashing red lights and has an extended stop arm. Additionally, passing should be avoided when approaching a hill or curve with limited visibility.

Question 6 - Practice Test 3

(D) When there are no traffic signals present, drivers must slow down or come to a stop to yield to pedestrians in marked or unmarked crosswalks. Furthermore, when making left or right turns at an intersection, it is essential to give the right-of-way to pedestrians.

Question 7 - Practice Test 3

(B) Escape ramps are specifically designed on steep mountain grades to provide a safe means of stopping runaway vehicles without jeopardizing the well-being of occupants. These ramps utilize loose, soft material, often pea gravel, to gradually slow down the vehicle.

Question 8 - Practice Test 3

(C) If a driver behind you continuously flashes their headlights, it is best to avoid any confrontations and simply move out of their way.

Question 9 - Practice Test 3

(D) Avoid attempting to overtake another vehicle when you're nearing or crossing an intersection or crosswalk.

Question 10 - Practice Test 3

(D) Contrary to the last statement, bicycles and motorcycles, being smaller and harder to spot, can move and stop faster than expected.

Question 11 - Practice Test 3

(B) If your rear wheels start to skid, turn the steering wheel in the direction the vehicle is trying to go. Steer left if your rear wheels are sliding left, and steer right if they are sliding right. The rear wheels may overcorrect and begin skidding in the opposite direction; if this happens, turn the steering wheel in that direction as well. This method, known as "steering into the skid".

Question 12 - Practice Test 3

(A) If vehicles approach an intersection from opposite directions at approximately the same time, the vehicle turning left must yield to the vehicle proceeding straight or turning right.

Question 13 - Practice Test 3

(B) Pedestrians and vehicles already in an intersection have the right-of-way. Since a roundabout or rotary is a circular intersection, you must yield the right-of-way to pedestrians and vehicles already in the circle when entering.

Question 14 - Practice Test 3

(B) High beams allow you to see further ahead, but they can create glare by reflecting off fog, rain, or snow, making it harder to see. Use low beams in fog, rain, or snow.

Question 15 - Practice Test 3

(B) You cannot pass a vehicle on the left if your lane has a solid yellow centerline. Even if your lane has a broken yellow centerline, you may not pass on the left if you would be unable to return to the right lane

Question 16 - Practice Test 3

(A) Exit ramps allow vehicles to leave expressways. Speed limits are often reduced at exit ramps.

Question 17 - Practice Test 3

(D) If the street is too narrow for a U-turn, make a three-point turn to change your vehicle's direction. This maneuver should only be performed when the street is narrow, visibility is good, traffic is light on both sides, the turn is allowed, and no other option is available.

Question 18 - Practice Test 3

(C) A single standard alcoholic drink (1.5 ounces of liquor, 5 ounces of wine, or 12 ounces of beer) can raise your blood alcohol content (BAC) to 0.02% or higher. At a BAC of 0.02%, your ability to track a moving target visually and perform two tasks simultaneously is impaired.

Question 19 - Practice Test 3

(D) When another vehicle is passing you on the left, reduce your speed slightly and maintain your position in the center of your lane until the vehicle has safely passed and is ahead of you. Once the vehicle has safely passed, you can resume your normal speed.

Question 20 - Practice Test 3

(D) When turning right on a multi-lane road, you should generally use the rightmost lane, unless signs, signals, or lane markings permit turning from multiple lanes.

Question 21 - Practice Test 3

(C) You should not pass a vehicle on the right if it is making or about to make a right turn. Ensure the passing lane is clear before attempting to pass.

Question 22 - Practice Test 3

(A) When driving in open country at night, use your high-beam headlights, as they allow you to see much further than low beams.

Question 23 - Practice Test 3

(D) Tractor-trailers often appear to be moving slower than they actually are due to their large size. Maintain a safe distance and be cautious when passing or turning around them.

Question 24 - Practice Test 3

(D) Always look both ways at railroad crossings, crosswalks, and intersections. Be sure to follow the left-right-left rule to check for approaching pedestrians, vehicles, or trains.

Question 25 - Practice Test 3

(A) You should always signal before passing another vehicle to ensure safe and clear communication with other drivers on the road.

Question 26 - Practice Test 3

(A) Your horn should be used to warn pedestrians or other drivers of potential danger. However, avoid using your horn unnecessarily or to express anger at others, as this can be a sign of aggressive driving.

Question 27 - Practice Test 3

(D) The type of alcohol does not affect your BAC, as the amount of ethanol matters rather than the form it takes. All alcoholic drinks contain different amounts of ethanol, but 1.5 ounces of 80-proof liquor, 5 ounces of wine, 12 ounces of beer, and 12 ounces of wine cooler have the same amount of ethanol.

Question 28 - Practice Test 3

(C) As the driver, you are responsible for ensuring all children in the vehicle are properly secured. Fines and penalty points may apply for each violation.

Question 29 - Practice Test 3

(C) The appropriate hand signal for a right turn is a left arm bent at 90 degrees, pointing upward.

Question 30 - Practice Test 3

(C) Treat a flashing red light like a stop sign, meaning you must stop before entering the intersection, yield to traffic and pedestrians, and proceed when safe.

Question 31 - Practice Test 3

(A) Bridges, overpasses, and ramps are especially vulnerable to icing because they are exposed to more moisture and cold air. When driving on these surfaces in freezing weather, use caution.

Question 32 - Practice Test 3

(C) Vehicles already on the expressway have the right-of-way when a vehicle is merging.

Question 33 - Practice Test 3

(C) At an all-way stop, yield to vehicles that arrived before you. Vehicles should proceed in the order they arrived, with the first vehicle to arrive going first.

Question 34 - Practice Test 3

(C) Blind pedestrians have the absolute right-of-way. Yield to the pedestrian, stopping if necessary. Avoid honking your horn near a blind pedestrian, as it may startle them or mask essential auditory cues.

Question 35 - Practice Test 3

(B) It is likely safe to merge back in front of the vehicle once you can see its entire front bumper in your rear-view mirror.

Question 36 - Practice Test 3

(A) If you're stopped at an intersection and a vehicle is rapidly approaching from behind, it's advisable to edge your vehicle forward (without entering the intersection), offering the approaching vehicle more space to halt.

Question 37 - Practice Test 3

(D) The principal aids for a blind individual are a white cane or a trained guide dog. Always yield the right-of-way to blind pedestrians.

Question 38 - Practice Test 3

(C) The total stopping distance is made up of your perception distance (the distance your vehicle travels from the time your eyes see the hazard until your brain registers it), reaction distance (the distance your vehicle travels from the time your brain tells your foot to press the brake pedal until your foot begins to brake), and braking distance (the distance your vehicle continues to travel after you've applied the brake).

Question 39 - Practice Test 3

(D) When you're at a railroad crossing with only a stop sign, you should only proceed when it's clear that no train, pedestrian, or other potential hazards are approaching, ensuring it's safe to cross.

Question 40 - Practice Test 3

(A) To prevent highway hypnosis, a state of drowsiness induced by monotonous sounds and repetitive sights, regularly shift your gaze to different parts of the road and observe various objects. Regular cell phone use or changing lanes can be risky.

ROAD SIGNS

Question 1 - Road Signs

(A) The image illustrates that overtaking on the left is permissible when the road ahead is clear. Overtaking and passing should be done with caution due to oncoming traffic.

Question 2 - Road Signs

(D) This sign denotes that a rest area is available on the right.

Question 3 - Road Signs

(C) This warning sign indicates the presence of a playground ahead.

Question 4 - Road Signs

(A) This sign warns drivers that a nearby side road crosses a railroad track. When turning onto the side road, proceed with caution.

Question 5 - Road Signs

(C) This sign denotes that you are not permitted to park in a handicap zone unless you have the necessary permit.

Question 6 - Road Signs

(C) A vehicle with a reflective triangular orange sign on the rear identifies it as a low-speed or slow-moving vehicle, which is typically defined as a motor vehicle with a top speed of no more than 25 mph. Farm vehicles and road maintenance vehicles are examples of these type of slow-moving vehicles. Slow down and proceed with caution if you come across one of these vehicles.

Question 7 - Road Signs

(B) The blue-and-white signs direct you to services such as gas stations, fast food restaurants, motels, and hospitals. Picture B indicates that there is a hospital ahead.

Question 8 - Road Signs

(C) In this case the larger sign alerts you to the impending arrival of a speed zone. The speed limit is indicated by the smaller sign. The speed limit will be reduced to 45 mph ahead in this case. So be prepared to slow down so that you don't go over the speed limit.

Question 9 - Road Signs

(A) Typically, vertical rectangular signs provide instructions or inform you of traffic laws. Drivers, pedestrians, and cyclists are given instructions by such regulatory signs.

Question 10 - Road Signs

(C) This sign denotes that the road ahead curves in the direction indicated by the arrow.

Question 11 - Road Signals Full

(A) This is a warning sign that may be placed ahead of the railroad crossing. Vehicles must slow down, look, listen, and be prepared to stop at the crossing ahead.

Question 12 - Road Signs

(A) The sequential arrow panels can be used in work zones 24 hours a day, seven days a week. This sign indicates that the lane ahead is closed and that you should take the lane to your left.

Question 13 - Road Signs

(C) This sign denotes that the divided highway is ending ahead. The road will be converted to a two-way street. Keep to the right and keep an eye out for oncoming traffic.

Question 14 - Road Signs

(B) This sign is normally displayed at an intersection with a combination of signals, including a green arrow pointing left. When the green arrow is lit, you may make a protected left turn; oncoming traffic will be stopped at a red light. This sign indicates that if the green arrow disappears and a steady green light appears, you may still make a left turn, but you must now yield to oncoming traffic before turning.

Question 15 - Road Signs

(B) A disabled crossing is indicated by the sign ahead. Slow down and take your time.

Question 16 - Road Signs

(D) This indicates a warning signal. Bicyclists and pedestrians frequently cross the road in the vicinity of the sign. You must drive cautiously and be prepared to stop.

Question 17 - Road Signs

(B) This sign denotes a bicycle crossing. This sign forewarns you that a bikeway will cross the road ahead.

Question 18 - Road Signs

(C) If you see this sign while driving in the left lane, you should turn left at the next intersection.

Question 19 - Road Signs

(D) This warning sign indicates that there will be a double curve ahead. The road ahead bends to the right, then to the left. (A winding road sign would be posted instead if there was a triple curve ahead.) Slow down, stay to the right, and do not pass.

Question 20 - Road Signs

(D) The pedestrian signals are only used to direct pedestrian traffic. This pedestrian signal indicates that pedestrians may enter the crosswalk to cross the road. (Older signals displayed the word "WALK" instead.) A signal with an upraised hand warns pedestrians not to enter the crosswalk. (Older signals displayed the words "DO NOT WALK" instead.)

Question 21 - Road Signs

(A) This navigational sign indicates the presence of a hospital ahead.

Question 22 - Road Signs

(A) This symbol indicates an exit number. This is the number assigned to a highway exit at a junction. If an interchange has more than one exit, a letter may be added to indicate which exit it is: For example: 117A, 117B, and so on.

Question 23 - Road Signs

(A) This is a gas station service sign

Question 24 - Road Signs

(C) This is a speed advisory sign at a roundabout. In the roundabout, the speed limit is 15 mph.

Question 25 - Road Signs

(A) This is a traffic control sign. This sign indicates that traffic must only make a left turn.

Question 26 - Road Signs

(A) The arrow signifies a right turn. In contrast, a red slash inside a red circle symbolizes "no." Turning right is prohibited by this regulatory sign. This sign is typically located on the right side of the road or above a driving lane.

Question 27 - Road Signs

(B) This service sign indicates that a telephone service is available ahead.

Question 28 - Road Signs

(B) This sign indicates that you need to make a right turn ahead in order to enter or stay on Interstate 95. It is guiding you to follow the direction of the arrow to continue on the correct route.

Question 29 - Road Signs

(B) This sign shows the safest speed to enter or depart an expressway. Reduce your speed to the specified speed (in this case, 30 mph).

Question 30 - Road Signs

(B) A single broken (dashed) yellow line may exist on a two-lane, two-way road. Vehicles on either side may pass if it is safe to do so.

Question 31 - Road Signs

(D) Lane use control signs are rectangular, black-and-white signs that indicate whether or not turning from specific lanes is required at an intersection. You are only permitted to drive in the direction indicated for your traffic lane.

Question 32 - Road Signs

(B) This sign shows the presence of a four-way intersection ahead. Drivers should be alert for cross traffic entering the roadway.

Question 33 - Road Signs

(A) This sign indicates a low-ground clearance railroad crossing. The railroad crossing is elevated enough that a vehicle with a large wheelbase or limited ground clearance could become stranded on the tracks. A car driver should have no trouble navigating this type of railroad crossing unless he or she is towing a trailer or driving a mobile home with low ground clearance.

Question 34 - Road Signs

(B) If your lane has a broken or dashed line (white or yellow), you may pass if it is safe to do so.

Question 35 - Road Signs

(C) A stop sign is an eight-sided white-on-red sign that indicates other traffic has the right-of-way. Always come to a complete stop before proceeding and yield to approaching vehicles.

Question 36 - Road Signs

(D) Work zone signs notify drivers of unusual or potentially hazardous conditions on or around the traveled route. These signs include black lettering or symbols on an orange background. If you encounter these signals, slow down and pay close attention.

Question 37 - Road Signs

(A) The shape of the arrow indicates that you are going to enter a winding road. A winding road has at least three turns. Take your time and slow down.

Question 38 - Road Signs

(C) When the road surface is wet, it becomes slippery. This sign is frequently found near bridges and overpasses.

Question 39 - Road Signs

(B) This is a freeway interchange sign. This sign warns you that you are approaching an interchange.

Question 40 - Road Signs

(D) This sign indicates that you must never park on the left side of the sign.

Question 41 - Road Signs

(B) This sign advises that the road ahead will be divided into two lanes. To separate opposing lanes, a divider, also known as a median, will be used. Continue right.

Question 42 - Road Signs

(B) This sign indicates that you are driving in the wrong way. Turn around.

Question 43 - Road Signs

(D) This sign denotes that the maximum nighttime speed limit is 45 mph.

Question 44 - Road Signs

(A) This is an emergency vehicle warning sign. It indicates the possibility of emergency vehicles from fire stations or other emergency facilities entering the route. If an emergency vehicle approaches from any direction and is sounding a siren, blowing an air horn, or flashing lights, you must surrender to it.

Question 45 - Road Signs

(D) This sign can be located at the end of various T-intersections. It means that before turning right or left onto the through route, you must yield the right of way or come to a complete stop.

Question 46 - Road Signs

(C) This sign indicates that U-turns are not permitted in this area.

Question 47 - Road Signs

(B) This sign indicates a T-junction. This sign indicates that the road you're on is about to come to an end. Prepare to make a right or left turn. Yield to oncoming traffic.

Question 48 - Road Signs

(A) This is an animal crossing sign. In this area, the animal represented on the sign (in this case, a deer) is common. Keep a watch out for animals like this crossing the street, particularly at dawn and night. Deer, elk, and other species roam in herds. Keep an eye out for more if you spot one. A collision with a large animal has the potential to kill the animal, do significant damage to your vehicle.

Question 49 - Road Signs

(C) This sign warns drivers not to exceed the specified speed limit in a school zone or school crossing when there are children present. In this scenario, the maximum permissible speed is 15 mph.

Question 50 - Road Signs

(B) This sign is indicating a service. It is recommended that drivers use lodging facilities if necessary.

SIGNS AND SITUATIONS

permitted to use the lane.

Question 1 - Signs & Situations

(C) When parking downhill, you should turn your front wheels toward the curb. This ensures that if your car begins to roll, the curb will stop it from moving forward. Always engage the parking brake and leave the car in the appropriate gear (Park for automatic transmissions or Reverse for manual transmissions).

Question 2 - Signs & Situations

(C) If you come to an intersection where the traffic signals are not functioning, you should treat it as if there is a stop sign at each entrance, just like a four-way stop. This means you must come to a complete stop before entering the intersection, yield to other vehicles based on standard right-of-way rules, and proceed only when it is safe to do so, exercising great caution.

Question 3 - Signs & Situations

(D) This is a reserved lane. This lane is restricted to specific types of vehicles. High-occupancy vehicle (HOV) lanes and bus lanes are two examples. Keep an eye out for signs stating which cars are

Question 4 - Signs & Situations

(C) When two vehicles approach an intersection at roughly the same moment, the vehicle on the left must yield to the one on the right. In the absence of this rule, the vehicle turning left must yield to approaching traffic. Car A must yield to Car B in this situation.

Question 5 - Signs & Situations

(A) If your brakes fail while driving downhill, the vehicle may begin to roll forward. You can configure the transmission to counteract this movement. Set your manual transmission to Reverse. Set the automatic transmission to Park if you have one.

Question 6 - Signs & Situations

(C) At an uncontrolled intersection, a vehicle must yield to pedestrians in a marked or unmarked crosswalk. After considering pedestrians, each vehicle must yield to the one on its right. Consequently, Vehicle C must yield to Vehicle B, and Vehicle A must yield to Vehicle C.

Question 7 - Signs & Situations

(D) Lane use control signals are special overhead signals that indicate which lanes of a roadway may be utilized in various directions at different times. A flashing yellow "X" denotes that this lane is solely for left turns.

Question 8 - Signs & Situations

(C) If your vehicle's brakes fail while parked uphill, it may start rolling backward. To counter this movement, set your transmission accordingly. For manual transmissions, set it to first gear for maximum forward torque. For automatic transmissions, set it to Park.

Question 9 - Signs & Situations

(B) Always follow directions from a police officer, even if it means disregarding other traffic devices or rules. For example, drive through a red light or stop sign if a police officer waves you through.

Question 10 - Signs & Situations

(B) Consider a flashing red signal to be a STOP sign. That is, you must come to a complete stop before crossing the intersection, yield to oncoming vehicles and pedestrians, and then proceed cautiously when it is safe to do so.

Question 11 - Signs & Situations

(C) This sign suggests that the recommended speed for navigating the upcoming curve is 35 mph. The sign does not provide any details regarding the curve's angle.

Question 12 - Signs & Situations

(A) You must come to a complete stop and yield to all traffic and pedestrians ahead. You can then proceed when the intersection is clear and there are no vehicles approaching that may present a hazard.

Question 13 - Signs & Situations

(A) High-occupancy vehicle (HOV) lanes are designed for vehicles with multiple occupants. This sign means that this lane is an HOV 2+ lane, which requires at least two occupants in each vehicle. In other words, a driver and at least one passenger. An HOV 3+ lane would require a driver and at least two passengers.

Question 14 - Signs & Situations

(A) When two vehicles arrive at an uncontrolled intersection about the same time, the vehicle on the left must yield. Car A must yield in this situation.

Question 15 - Signs & Situations

(C) After yielding to all pedestrians and vehicles already in the junction, you can proceed on a green signal.

Question 16 - Signs & Situations

(A) If you have a green light, you may continue through the intersection, but you must first yield to all pedestrians and vehicles already in the intersection. In this case, Car A must yield to Car B since Car B has already entered the intersection.

Question 17 - Signs & Situations

(C) Prior to making a left turn off the road, you must yield to all pedestrians and oncoming traffic.

Question 18 - Signs & Situations

(D) Roads are typically at their slipperiest during the first 30 minutes of rain because the water mixes with dirt, oil, and other substances on the road, creating a slick surface. This condition will persist until more rain washes away these materials. Additionally, using cruise control on wet, icy, or snowy roads can be dangerous because it may cause your vehicle to lose traction, increasing the risk of a skid.

Question 19 - Signs & Situations

(D) At a STOP sign, you must stop before the stop line. If there isn't a stop line, stop before the crosswalk. If there isn't a crosswalk either, stop before entering the intersection.

Question 20 - Signs & Situations

(B) You may turn left on a green light after yielding to pedestrians, oncoming vehicles, and vehicles already in the intersection.

Question 21 - Signs & Situations

(A) When parking uphill parallel to a curb, point your wheels away from the curb and allow your vehicle to roll back slightly so the rear part of the front wheel on the curb side rests against the curb. If your brakes fail, the curb will prevent your car from rolling backward. Ensure you still engage your parking brake and leave your car in the appropriate gear.

Question 22 - Signs & Situations

(A) The sign displayed is a yield sign. When you encounter a yield sign, you should slow down and be ready to yield to both pedestrians and oncoming traffic. It's important to note that you may need to stop if there are pedestrians or vehicles that have the right of way.

Question 23 - Signs & Situations

(A) The driver intends to turn left.

Question 24 - Signs & Situations

(A) A flashing yellow traffic signal means that you should slow down and proceed with caution.

Question 25 - Signs & Situations

(C) If your turn signals and brake lights aren't working, try hand and arm signals. An arm pointing downward is a signal to slow down or stop.

FINE & LIMITS

Question 1 - Fines & Limits

(A) Children who are 7 or younger must be seated in a car seat in the back seat of the vehicle to minimize the risk from airbags in case of an accident.

Question 2 - Fines & Limits

(C) A Temporary Alcohol License (TAL) remains valid while you're waiting for the outcome of your hearing if you filed for it within 30 days of an Implied Consent or Blood Alcohol Concentration (BAC) charge. The current fee for a TAL is $100.

Question 3 - Fines & Limits

(D) A first-time DUI conviction will result in a license suspension for six months, and you may also face fines ranging from $400 to $1,000, plus court costs and a possible jail term of 48 hours to 30 days.

Question 4 - Fines & Limits

(B) You may be eligible for a conditional driver's license if you are at least 15½ years old and have met all the necessary requirements, including passing the vision and skills tests.

Question 5 - Fines & Limits

(B) In South Carolina, you're not allowed to stop or park within 20 feet of an intersection's crosswalk.

Question 6 - Fines & Limits

(C) Drivers under the age of 21 who are found guilty of operating a vehicle with a blood alcohol content (BAC) of 0.02% or greater within a five-year period will have their licenses suspended for three months for the first offense and six months for any subsequent offenses.

Question 7 - Fines & Limits

(A) If you fail the driving skills test on your first or second try, you have to wait for two weeks before taking it again.

Question 8 - Fines & Limits

(A) Refusal to submit to chemical tests for drugs or alcohol results in an immediate six-month license suspension for drivers of any age.

Question 9 - Fines & Limits

(C) If you haven't broken any traffic laws or been at fault in any accidents, you can obtain a conditional or special limited license when you reach 17 or after you've had it for a year.

Question 10 - Fines & Limits

(B) If you are found guilty of using illegal drugs while driving and it was your first offense, you might face a fine of $400 to $1,000 in addition to court fees. Additionally, you can receive a jail term of between 48 hours and 30 days. Your driver's license can be revoked for six months. Finally, if you use or possess drugs, you could face additional criminal consequences.

DISTRACTED DRIVING

Question 1 - Distracted Driving

(B) It is preferable to use a hands-free or speaker phone while driving if you are an adult driver and absolutely must use your phone. In several states, it is illegal and not advised to use a mobile phone while driving.

Question 2 - Distracted Driving

(C) Never turn around to attend to the needs of passengers, kids, or animals while you are driving. Pull over to the side of the road and park your vehicle if you need to attend to any passengers or animals.

Question 3 - Distracted Driving

(A) Although stimulants, physical activity, and music can help you stay alert, sleeping is the greatest cure for fatigue. Consult a doctor if, despite receiving 9 hours of sleep, you still feel exhausted.

Question 4 - Distracted Driving

(D) Before taking a medication, look for any warnings about its effect(s) while you are driving. Ask your doctor or pharmacist about any potential side effects if you are unsure if it is safe to take the medication and drive. Drugs used to treat headaches, colds, hay fever or other allergies, or to calm nerves might cause drowsiness and have an impact on a person's ability to drive. Similar to how alcohol does, some prescription medications can impair your reflexes, judgment, eyesight, and awareness.

Question 5 - Distracted Driving

(C) Many over-the-counter and prescription drugs might make you sleepy. Only use drugs while driving if your doctor says they won't impair your ability to drive safely.

Question 6 - Distracted Driving

(D) Texting while driving currently accounts for 25% of all car accidents in the US and is the greatest cause of death for youths. Texting while driving is illegal.

Question 7 - Distracted Driving

(A) Talking on a cell phone while driving increases your chances of being in a crash by up to four times. This is because the talk is taking your focus away from driving. Sending text messages (texting) while driving increases your chances of being in an accident by up to eightfold.

Question 8 - Distracted Driving

(D) Cell phones are not permitted to be used by underage drivers while driving, unless to notify an emergency.

Question 9 - Distracted Driving

(D) Distractions, even on straight roads or empty roads, should be avoided. Refrain from eating, drinking, smoking, texting, reading, or engaging in difficult conversations while driving. If possible, turn off your phone and keep it off until you have completed driving for the day.

Question 10 - Distracted Driving

(D) Fatigue can impair your judgment, slow down your reaction times, and decrease your awareness of your surroundings.

Question 11 - Distracted Driving

(D) Distractions while driving include text messaging, talking on the phone, dealing with children, and lighting a cigarette, among other activities that draw your attention away from the road.

Question 12 - Distracted Driving

(D) It is risky to do anything while driving that diverts your attention from the road, including getting dressed, putting on makeup, reading, eating, or drinking. Take care not to hold someone in your lap, or a pet or parcel in your arms.

Question 13 - Distracted Driving

(B) Highway hypnosis or drowsiness while driving can result from monotonous road and traffic conditions, the hum of wind, tires, and the engine. Drivers can avoid highway hypnosis by continuously moving their eyes and monitoring traffic and road signs around them.

Question 14 - Distracted Driving

(D) Activities that require the use of your hands should be avoided while driving. Listening to the radio, however, can help you stay alert.

Question 15 - Distracted Driving

(B) It is against the law for minors to use a cell phone while driving. If a cell phone rings, they should not answer the call. Violators of this law may face fines.

Question 16 - Distracted Driving

(C) You should set up your cab before starting your trip, but eating and drinking should be done at rest stops.

Question 17 - Distracted Driving

(A) Driving while operating a visual screen device or texting is illegal and prohibited by law.

Question 18 - Distracted Driving

(D) You should also be aware of potential distractions and impairments, as they can affect your driving abilities. All the listed factors, including emotional and physical states like fatigue, anger, illness, stress, and fear, can impair your driving skills.

DRINKING AND DRIVING

Question 1 - Drinking and Driving

(A) You should arrange for a designated driver to take you home if you've consumed too much alcohol to drive safely. A designated driver is someone who abstains from drinking and is responsible for driving others who have been drinking.

Question 2 - Drinking and Driving

(A) Only time can effectively eliminate alcohol from a person's system. Coffee and fresh air might alleviate some symptoms of intoxication but will not reduce the actual level of impairment.

Question 3 - Drinking and Driving

(D) Upon conviction of driving under the influence of alcohol or drugs, penalties may include license suspension, significant fines, and community service.

Question 4 - Drinking and Driving

(A) Alcohol consumption impairs vision, slows reactions, and affects judgment but does not increase alertness.

Question 5 - Drinking and Driving

(D) A standard serving of alcohol is typically 1.5 ounces, regardless of the type of drink.

Question 6 - Drinking and Driving

(C) Drinking alcohol and driving at night is especially risky because vision is already restricted due to darkness.

Question 7 - Drinking and Driving

(D) The type of alcohol does not affect blood alcohol concentration, as standard servings of different types of alcohol contain the same amount of alcohol.

Question 8 - Drinking and Driving

(D) Even small amounts of alcohol can impair a driver's reflexes, driving skills, and depth perception.

Question 9 - Drinking and Driving

(D) License suspension is mandatory for minors convicted of driving under the influence of drugs or transporting an open container of any alcoholic beverage.

Question 10 - Drinking and Driving

(B) Drunk driving is the leading cause of death among young Americans aged 16 to 24, with alcohol-related crashes occurring every 33 minutes.

Question 11 - Drinking and Driving

(D) Open containers of alcohol are only allowed in areas inaccessible to drivers or passengers, such as trunks, cargo areas, or truck beds.

Question 12 - Drinking and Driving

(D) Alcohol can impact your concentration, reaction time, and judgment.

Question 13 - Drinking and Driving

(D) Consuming alcohol before or while driving can diminish a driver's reflexes, physical control of the vehicle, and awareness of potential dangers on the road.

Question 14 - Drinking and Driving

(A) Drivers under 21 are not permitted to buy, consume, or possess alcohol.

Question 15 - Drinking and Driving

(A) The liver can process approximately one standard drink per hour. If you consume a large amount of alcohol, it may take a day or two for your body to fully recover.

Question 16 - Drinking and Driving

(A) Open container laws prohibit open containers of alcohol in areas accessible to the driver or passengers of a vehicle, with exceptions for limousines, taxis, motor homes, and commercial buses.

Question 17 - Drinking and Driving

(D) If you plan to drink alcohol, consider using public transportation, a taxi, or designating a sober driver to get home safely.

Question 18 - Drinking and Driving

(D) Drivers under the influence of alcohol are more likely to drive too fast or too slow, change lanes frequently, and fail to dim headlights.

Question 19 - Drinking and Driving

(D) Alcohol enters the bloodstream and affects various bodily processes, such as coordination, self-control, and reaction time. The only way to counteract alcohol's impact on the brain is to wait for it to leave the bloodstream.

Question 20 - Drinking and Driving

(A) The amount of alcohol a person can consume before reaching the legal limit varies from one individual to another and is influenced by several factors, such as body weight, metabolism, and tolerance.

MOCK TEST PRACTICE

.

Question 1 - Mock Exam

(D) Start from the lane that is closest to your intended direction. For a left turn from a two-way street, position your vehicle near the intersection's center and wait with your wheels straight until it's safe to complete the turn. Stay slightly to the left of the center as you make the turn. For a right turn, start in the rightmost lane and stay as close to the curb as possible.

Question 2 - Mock Exam

(D) Before crossing an intersection, you should check for vehicles approaching from both the left and right, as well as any pedestrians crossing. Look in both directions again just before moving. Also, observe the entire intersection to ensure it's clear.

Question 3 - Mock Exam

(C) When executing a left turn at an intersection with traffic controls, always yield to oncoming vehicles and pedestrians who are in the crosswalk or intersection.

Question 4 - Mock Exam

(B) A road with a Do Not Enter sign displayed is off-limits to traffic. Such notices will be posted at road openings that you shouldn't enter or where driving the wrong way on a one-way street would be unsafe. These signs can be found in several places on one-way streets, in crossovers on divided highways, and at exit ramps.

Question 5 - Mock Exam

(C) Pass no vehicle in a roundabout with many lanes. Be ready to stop for cars turning from the inner lane to the roundabout in front of you. Use the right lane if you want to leave the roundabout before it is halfway around.

Question 6 - Mock Exam

(C) There are several roads that have a solid white line indicating the correct margins. Only traffic heading to or from the shoulder is allowed to cross this line, which represents the outer boundary of the road. A solid yellow line serves as the other edge's marking.

Question 7 - Mock Exam

(C) Do not attempt to overtake another vehicle while you're approaching or traversing an intersection or crosswalk.

Question 8 - Mock Exam

(B) You're required to inform the SCDMV within 10 days if you change your name or address. Name changes must be done in person with proper documentation, while address changes can be made online or in person.

Question 9 - Mock Exam

(D) Warning signs are posted to alert drivers of potential dangers ahead, encouraging them to proceed cautiously. These signs often feature black text or symbols on a yellow background.

Question 10 - Mock Exam

(D) A route-restricted driver's license allows you to travel to and from specific locations like school, work, and court-mandated drug or alcohol programs, including Alcohol and Drug Safety Action Program (ADSAP).

Question 11 - Mock Exam

(D) Behaviors like cutting off or swerving in front of other vehicles, excessive honking, tailgating, and forcing a car off the road are all signs of road rage.

Question 12 - Mock Exam

(D) When slowing down or coming to a stop, you should use either brake-operated signal lights or hand signals to alert the driver behind you.

Question 13 - Mock Exam

(D) When navigating through city traffic, aim to look at least one block ahead. Generally, this covers about a 10-second span.

Question 14 - Mock Exam

(A) Colored curb markings can be used in place of or in addition to regulation signs to limit parking. You cannot park there if the curb is painted yellow in South Carolina, except for loading or unloading for a brief time.

Question 15 - Mock Exam

(C) Rear-end collisions are the most common type of accident on interstate highways. Tailgating is frequently the cause, and it's advised to maintain a safe following distance of three to four seconds under normal driving conditions.

Question 16 - Mock Exam

(A) On a narrow mountain road where neither vehicle can pass, the downhill vehicle must yield the right-of-way by backing up so that the uphill vehicle can move ahead. The downhill-facing vehicle generally has better control while backing up.

Question 17 - Mock Exam

(D) Under South Carolina law, you are required to present your driver's license, vehicle registration, and proof of insurance to the police officer when stopped for a traffic violation or equipment check.

Question 18 - Mock Exam

(B) A steady red arrow signal indicates you must come to a complete stop and are not allowed to proceed in the arrow's direction until it changes to green.

Question 19 - Mock Exam

(C) Only the passage of time can sober you up. Your body typically metabolizes about one ounce of alcohol per hour, and this rate cannot be sped up by coffee, food, or a cold shower.

Question 20 - Mock Exam

(B) In South Carolina, you are required to parallel park within 18 inches of the curb. Failing to do so can be hazardous to other road users.

Question 21 - Mock Exam

(D) While driving, adjusting your seat, mirrors, or radio can cause you to lose focus. You should make any necessary modifications before you begin to drive.

Question 22 - Mock Exam

(D) A slower speed limit is typically posted in a work zone. Otherwise, adhere to the standard speed restriction. A conviction for speeding in a construction zone in South Carolina carries a fine of $500 to $1,000 as well as two points on the driver's record.

Question 23 - Mock Exam

(A) If your gas pedal sticks, put your car into neutral. This will disconnect the engine from the wheels, allowing you to safely stop the car.

Question 24 - Mock Exam

(D) At an intersection, your first look should be to the left since cars coming from that direction will be closer to you.

Question 25 - Mock Exam

(B) Pull your car entirely off the travelled area of the road if you need to make an emergency stop on a road or highway. Afterward, caution other drivers. Lift your car's hood and activate your danger (four-way) flashers. Attach a piece of fabric to the handle of the driver's side door. If you have any warning signs, such flares or reflective triangles, get out of your car on the passenger side and place them 200 to 300 feet behind it.

Question 26 - Mock Exam

(A) You should look in the front, sides, and rear before starting to back up, and you should keep looking in the rear as you do so. Be wary of your mirrors because they have blind spots.

Question 27 - Mock Exam

(A) Unless signs, signals, or pavement markings state otherwise, you should keep close to the curb when making a right turn. The car in front of you might attempt to pass you on the right if you make a wide left turn, giving the impression that you are genuinely making a left turn. That might result in a collision.

Question 28 - Mock Exam

(A) Two solid yellow lines cannot be crossed in order to pass or change lanes. To turn left, though, you may cross the lines.

Question 29 - Mock Exam

(D) If your license was suspended for one of the following infractions and you requested an administrative hearing within 30 days, you can be qualified for a temporary alcohol license (TAL): BAC of 0.15% - BAC of 0.02% or greater under 21 - Implied Consent - Implied Consent under 21

Question 30 - Mock Exam

(D) If your vehicle breaks down and can't be moved completely off the road, stop where it is visible from a distance to trailing vehicles. Avoid stopping over hills or around curves where your car might not be seen.

Made in the USA
Columbia, SC
24 November 2024

47448093R00100